WHY NOT ME?

MASCOT
BOOKS

www.mascotbooks.com

Why Not Me?

I have tried to recreate events, locales, and conversations from my memories of them. In order to maintain their anonymity in some instances I have changed the names of individuals and places. I may have changed some identifying characteristics and details such as physical properties, occupations, and places of residence.

For more information, please contact:
Mascot Books
620 Herndon Parkway #320
Herndon, VA 20170
info@mascotbooks.com

Library of Congress Control Number: 2021901183

CPSIA Code: PRV0921B
ISBN-13: 978-1-64543-880-9

Printed in the United States

FOR YOU

WHY NOT ME?

BORN TO FAIL DESTINED TO SUCCEED

A MEMOIR ABOUT DEFYING THE ODDS

TODD M. SIMMONS

I WANT TO TELL YOU about the title of this book, *Why Not Me?* As you'll see, it's a question I want you to ask yourself, as well. For many years I asked this question from a place of negativity—looking at what I didn't start out with, what I didn't have, and what I couldn't be. I expected to live a life of mediocrity at best, or at worst, something called *the fast life*—where you either end up locked up or dead. There are people in my life who went that direction, and it always amazes me how I escaped the chain of events that ensnared them. I escaped the mediocrity that I've seen others fall into; it's a monotony that can be like death.

Thankfully, I was blessed that my life took a different turn of events. The Roman philosopher Seneca once said, "Luck is what happens when preparation meets opportunity," and I believe this describes how I got to where I am today. Over the course of my life, I have met individuals who changed my perspective, gave me the tough love I needed, and opened up doors—and I didn't just walk through them. I charged through them because deep down inside, I have always wanted to achieve something more.

I joined the United States Air Force and worked my way up through the ranks, eventually leading its educational branch. Along the way, I faced adversarial forces in my immediate surroundings and even ones that came at me from my past. Race, education, family, and mental health all presented hurdles I needed to clear in order to get to where I am today.

I grew up in an underserved, southern community that was lacking in resources. Among the things it lacked, and perhaps the most significant, was education. Added to this environment was a dysfunctional family and a culture that not only espoused but glorified drama and sometimes violence. It was a narrow escape for me to emerge unscathed, and I give credit to individuals along the way who saw something more inside of me or encouraged me to be my best self.

But my challenges didn't stop once I graduated high school; they continued to come my way even as I moved into military life. From outward experiences of racism in the ranks to inward experiences of stress and depression, I've had personal and professional challenges continue to present opportunities for growth, and, well, here I am today. I want to share my story with you. Because you know what? Everyone has challenges in life. They may not be the same challenges that I went through, and I may not go through the challenges that you went through, but we have this in common: If we're going to be our best selves, we have to ask ourselves, *Why not me*?

As I grew older and wiser from the challenges that life brought my way, I learned to ask the question of *Why not me?* from a different angle. One of positivity. One of hope. One of empowerment. Why not me for this opportunity, or to reach that goal, or to be that person I didn't think I could be? And by the time you're done reading my story, I want you to ask the same question of yourself from that same positive place.

But before we get there, I want to take you back to the beginning . . .

1

Don't let your struggle become your identity.
—Unknown

I WAS SIX YEARS OLD when our house burned down. To this day, I can remember that smell, and anytime I smell burning wood, I'm taken back to that memory. It all started with an incorrectly installed gas heater in our den. Our neighbor saw smoke coming from the house. She described it as beautiful smoke coming from the chimney, like a fire had been lit on purpose, and we were all cozy around the hearth. So she came over to check it out, and she saw that our house was actually on fire. Thankfully, nobody was home. My mom was actually at the utility company paying the monthly bill when she overheard the request for someone to come turn the power off at a house that burned. She had no idea they were talking about our home. The cause of the fire was ruled a faulty gas heater. To this day, I have a fear of using gas or propane-powered devices.

When the fire department came, they used water to put out the fire, of course. Between the fire damage and the water damage, our home was totaled. I remember my mom crying hysterically. Even at that young age, I could feel her devastation. One of the only areas that emerged unscathed was the front closet and the jackets in there; I remember my mom taking them out. She had owned this house after purchasing it with her first husband. It was a source of pride for her, and with that fire she felt like she lost everything.

That's how we ended up in a trailer next to the church we attended. I grew up in a small town near the coast of South Carolina. We attended a small Baptist church, where most of my mom's family was from. Once slavery had ended, many of them acquired land and started farms. Our house that had burned down was in a populated section of town, where I had friends and saw people. Now we were living in a completely different area. It was just the trailer and the church. I think this is where my very active imagination began. It was a yellow single-wide trailer with two or three bedrooms. Our new home was very isolated. There was the church, the cemetery, and then the trailer—right across the street from a lake that was used for baptisms. I remember riding the bus home one day, and the driver had no idea where she was dropping me off. She couldn't believe we lived there. I remember a certain fear would come into me as I looked through our windows at the cemetery, especially at night.

Not everyone in our family lived there. I was often going back and forth to my great-grandmother's house. I was the youngest of four children. I had a brother ten years older than me, a sister who was eight years older, and another sister who was seven years older.

My two sisters, Leslie and Katrina, and my brother, Eric, were from a different father. My father was a man my mom had met after she had gotten divorced from my siblings' father. Nobody ever really sat me down to explain all this—it was just something I sort of learned over time. I think it's one of the biggest reasons I always felt different, and that feeling permeated my childhood memories. For one thing, I grew up thinking my siblings hated me. As a young child, I didn't know how to process that. I was almost a decade younger than my siblings. Their father was not really involved in their lives, and I felt as though my presence may have caused some resentment or contributed to my mother divorcing their father. My mother really overcompensated in protecting me. I think she felt some guilt, which she tried to shield me from.

During the 1980s, every family had an *Encyclopedia Britannica* in their house. My sisters and older cousins used to open the encyclopedia up to the entry about George Washington. My last name was Simmons; theirs was Washington. They always told me about how George Washington was their grandfather, how he did this, and how he did that. Well, knowing American history, I suppose there could be some element of truth to them being related to Washington, but he definitely wasn't their grandfather. They were just creating this narrative to make me feel inferior.

Words were rough, and nobody minced them in my family—we had to have thick skin. My siblings repeatedly called me a bastard in my earlier years. It took me years to learn the meaning of the term. There was no Google back then, so one day I looked it up in the dictionary. I think it still took a little bit of time to sink in. When I learned what it meant, I asked my mom why she wasn't married to my father. She brushed off my question by saying, "I love you, and that's all that matters." It did sting a little bit, especially because that insult got all wrapped up in the confusion of my dad shuffling in and out of my life. Around the age of seven or eight, my older sister Katrina and I developed a better relationship. My mom was working a lot, my older brother had moved out, and my second sister was living with a relative. My sister became a surrogate mother to me. By the age of nine, she was dating a man who would become her future husband at eighteen. This was also a life-changing time for me, as my future brother-in-law, Jonathan, became the first constant, positive male role model in my life. Until then, I really did not have any consistent male role models. This relationship remains one of the strongest in my life. I credit him with showing me the value of hard work, taking care of my family, and opening my eyes to the larger world outside my small town.

Once I became an adult, I developed a closer relationship with all my siblings. I was just a kid, so I didn't know how to process their specific brand of bullying. I felt like everyone was always looking at me as if there were some secret I didn't know.

It wasn't until I became an adult that I realized the

influence my childhood had on the rest of my life. But my siblings weren't just rough with their words. They used to join forces with my cousins to smother me with a pillow. To be fair, they used to do that kind of stuff to each other, but I was the youngest one in the house by almost a decade. Sometimes they would smother me to the point of placing me in a severe panic. To this day, I can't tolerate anything over my face, putting my head underwater, or being in a confined space.

These insults and bullying and the less-than-us narrative led me to develop the idea that I was hated, and that led to numbness. I became somewhat of a reclusive individual at a young age. I would hide under my mom's bed for hours at a time. Sometimes people noticed I was not around, and sometimes they did not. That spot under the bed became a place of refuge for me and made me feel secure. I believed that's why even today I enjoy my own company or have the ability to sit peacefully in silence with my own thoughts. There was also a pervading sense that my life was some sort of secret. Even though we lived in a small town, people were routinely confused about who my parents were. They often didn't know I was the son of my mother, and they thought my siblings' father was also my father.

I never thought much of it, but I stopped caring about myself. I became reckless, acting with abandon and ignoring the consequences. This led to poor academic performance at school. I didn't fear authority. I didn't turn in my homework. I remember being in the fourth grade, and my teacher was a young White woman who was not from our community. She was new to teaching, and I can vividly remember her struggling to keep control of the class. In a way, I tried to not be disruptive, but I think I just fell in with the crowd. I would do crazy stuff, like running into a wall to see what it would feel like to break my arm. I am not sure if this constitutes an early sign of trauma, but these are the first memories I have of pushing the limits and experiencing thoughts of harming myself. I think I wanted to feel something.

One time we took a table and made a ramp. I jumped my bicycle off it and had a horrific fall. I had to be carried home, where I laid in bed temporarily paralyzed. I think it had shocked my nerves. I would shoot pellet guns, and they would ricochet around our yard and hit me in the forehead, but I didn't care. I was frequently left home alone after my oldest sister married and left home, so I would get into doing stupid stuff. Even with my friends, I tried crazy things. This fearlessness—or really, this numbness, this apathy, this lack of care about life and its consequences—proved harmful as I got older.

Before our house burned down, my great-uncle introduced my mom to the new pastor of our church. He had been trying to bring the pastor into town from Ohio, and he thought this fellow and my mom would be a good match. The pastor was a tall, slender man, older than my mom by about ten years. He looked very distinguished, and he was quiet and conservative about everything he did. I don't remember anything he preached about, but I do remember he did a lot of traveling to other churches.

About a year after our house had burned down, we moved into a brand-new home that was built on the ashes of our old house. Only now, my mom had married the pastor, and she was moving into the house and taking care of five kids because the pastor had moved in with his teenage son.

It was a turbulent time, and I felt this constant tension in the house. The pastor expected a lot. I remember how he would sit and read his newspaper in a suit, and my mom would cook for him. It was like he expected her to cater to him. I don't know what it was exactly, but I felt a lot of uneasiness when he was around. I remember one time he took me to McDonald's when he got his car washed. He drove a late 1970s gray Lincoln—the kind of car you'd expect a Black southern preacher to drive. We sat there eating our food. I can't tell you today what was running through my young mind, but he just made me uneasy.

The new house had three bedrooms. With five kids and two adults under the same roof, I became the odd man out. My oldest brother and the pastor's son turned out to be the same age. They had twin beds, and I had a pullout bed. Sharing a room with two sixteen-year-old boys meant that I wasn't really in the room. I would sleep in different places, like the room my sisters shared. I would snore, and they would put me in the hallway. I just didn't feel like I had anywhere to go, and I wondered why I wasn't worthy of equal treatment.

This alienation drove me into my imagination. I was constantly dreaming and daydreaming. I would daydream to the point where it would obscure reality. Everything was pretend. I inundated myself with books and television. I'd see how things were in exotic places like Indonesia and Africa—worlds I didn't even know existed—and they certainly didn't in my own neighborhood.

Hardeeville, South Carolina, where we lived, was sandwiched between Hilton Head Island and Savannah, right on the border between Georgia and South Carolina. Hilton Head was full of millionaires, vacationers, and just generally a lot of folks coming to soak up the southern sun. Savannah was full of southern history. If someone flew into Savannah to go to Hilton Head, they drove through Hardeeville, a small town of about six thousand people.

Hardeeville wasn't a very wealthy place. Many of the people there worked in the service industry at the hotels along the beach on Hilton Head. It was just a thing: people grew up and got jobs in Hilton Head. A lot of my own family provided labor to the resorts there. Both of my parents worked in the service industry for decades. My mom cleaned villas and worked in several resort restaurants. It is actually where she met my dad in the mid-1970s. My dad worked in the restaurant business for forty or fifty years, thirty of which were spent at the same restaurant. To this day, I have never stepped foot in that restaurant, even though he still works there. It's only twenty minutes away from my mom's house, but I've never received an invitation to bring my family there.

My parents would work mornings in the restaurant and then banquets in the evening at the hotels. They were working twelve to fourteen hours a day. Sometimes my mom would stay in Hilton Head overnight, so I would stay with my great-grandmother. I didn't see my own father much during this time. As it turns out, my mother and my father had never gotten married. He was around here and there, but he didn't really put his time into my family.

He was in and out for the first eighteen years of my life. Our relationship was fractured. Growing up, he was present one or two days a week when he and my mom were together. My dad didn't talk about his personal life. I knew he grew up without parents, but I found out later he actually had a bigger family. He was a Vietnam vet, and he had been drafted into the United States Marine Corps.

When I was sixteen or seventeen years old, he would come in around nine or ten at night, maybe with some alcohol on his breath. After routinely smoking a joint, he would tell me stories about Vietnam. We talked about weapons he had fired and strange encounters he had experienced. Our relationship was always standoffish, though.

I saw my dad once or twice a week but never on holidays. By contrast, my mom had seven sisters, so family get-togethers were big around the holidays. But my dad wasn't a part of the picture.

I would always rationalize it. I would create narratives, like maybe he was working late all the time. But after I turned fourteen or fifteen, I stopped rationalizing his absence. I decided that maybe he didn't care. One slight thing that connected us was the routine of getting ready for school before the fall—things like getting school clothes. But that stopped in ninth grade, and I started taking care of myself. With him no longer even helping out with things like that, our contact diminished even further.

Later on in life, when I was in the military, I found out he had another family eighty-nine miles away—a wife, a son one year younger than me, and a daughter one year older—and that kind of put it all into perspective for me. It started with my mom telling me I had a brother in the air force. From there, I did some research to find him. Once I had his name, it was pretty easy to track him down. I remember looking him up in our global email system and seeing his name for the first time. My heart started beating really fast, and then I knew it was real. I actually had a younger brother with my last name serving in the air force. How crazy is that? I got a better sense of why he wasn't around, or why I kept having this inner feeling that I wasn't a priority in his life. I did make contact with both of my paternal siblings when I was twenty-eight. My brother and I conversed off and on for a few years, but my sister never wanted to meet me or have any interaction. I think the idea of our father having a second family was too much for her. I have to be honest: the cold shoulder took me back to the feelings I had when I was young and felt like my older siblings hated and resented me. I did ask the question: What did I do? I certainly did not ask to be in this situation. I felt like a complete outcast and even more disconnected. To this day, I have not met either one of them in person.

My older siblings' father was not super involved in their lives, either. When they were young, he picked them up a handful of times and took them fishing. As a young kid, I wanted to go too. I didn't really understand why I couldn't come along, but it started to make sense over the years. I never met any of my four grandparents—they had all passed away before I was born. My mom was gone a lot during this time, too.

My great-grandmother was a stable presence in my life. She was alive until I was nineteen. She was sort of like the matriarch in our family. I spent a lot of time at her house, which we nicknamed backstreet. We usually called her Momma. She took care of everyone. Her house was a safe place not only for me, but for many family members who frequently needed a place to stay or change. It was like a mini hotel, sometimes. She always had food on the stove, a fire lit, and an open door. It was also a family meeting place. We would draw names for Christmas at her house. She was definitely the glue back then.

When I was at my great-grandma's house, I would read through the family Bible, which had our family record going back to the 1800s—all the deaths and births in our family. I learned that we had a proud history with a lot of business owners. For example, my grandfather was one of the first Black men to own his own logging business in South Carolina since the 1930s. Momma had old receipts, telegrams, and medals from my uncle, who was killed in Vietnam when he was just nineteen. Though he died young, he had already married, and his son never got to meet him. I honored my uncle at my military retirement. As a tribute to his service, I gave his son the flag that was given to me so that he could connect with the father he had never met. I routinely visit the Vietnam memorial wall in Washington, DC, where his name and the names of over fifty-eight thousand patriots who gave the ultimate sacrifice are engraved. I have taken countless friends and family to this sacred spot.

My great-grandmother also had the deed for the land that her house was on; it was our family's first piece of property. The documents were so old and faded that they were practically brown. Unfortunately, we lost this land when I was twenty-seven. After everything our ancestors had endured, it hurt to know that we lost that land over a few thousand dollars in taxes. In fact, the pain of it makes it hard for me to even pass by my great-grandmother's house whenever I'm in the area.

But those pieces of history were a source of pride for her. We had some candid conversations about our family history. It always amazed me how closely connected I was to slavery—just a few generations removed. The White family that our family was freed from lived within five miles of us and still came around to visit my great-uncle. Even some of the descendants of that family would come by and visit him at his farm into the 1980s and 1990s. For whatever reason, a connection still existed. I was young and could not fully understand the nature of the relationship, but I knew it was from a place of unspoken acknowledgement of kinship.

My great-grandmother had a picture of her father on the wall the entire time she lived in her house. His parents were slaves. That photograph was like something one would see in a movie about the Wild West. It was behind thick glass and set in a hand-carved oval wooden frame, all of it extremely heavy. It was a majestic portrait, really, with him in a suit looking distinguished and put together. Though it was a black-and-white photograph, I could tell he was of mixed race—a gentleman on the lighter side.

It was amazing that in 1990 I knew someone who knew someone who was alive during slavery. So, if I appreciated anything, I knew my lineage. We were freed, laid down roots, and opened businesses.

After we moved back into our new house, my mom went out and got wall-to-wall furniture. Everything was new. As for the pastor, her new husband, I never really got to know him. He never really spoke to me. In that entire year my mom was married to him, I can only recall one or two conversations. Eventually, the younger of my two sisters ended up moving out. I do not think we wanted the ready-made family he was now a part of.

Things continued to seem uneasy in the house. There was tension between my mom and my sister. Since the house had burned down and we had all been displaced, there was a lot of conflict within the family, like a wedge had been driven between us. When we did get back together, it just wasn't the same. People were already moving on down their own paths in life, leaving me behind.

One day, the pastor just left. He packed up his Lincoln and drove off, leaving behind a bunch of bills and his teenage son, who continued to stay with us. My mom had stopped working after she married him so she could be a pastor's wife and focus on traveling with him. He had been responsible for our finances. With him gone, she would need to go back to work. As it turned out, she needed a second job to keep the new house and new furniture she had bought, not to mention raising five kids who needed clothes and food.

That entire experience made me very skeptical of church and religion. Whenever I would meet a new pastor, any character flaw they might have would drive me away. But at that time, when I was a kid, the church played an important role in my life. My mom would take me to church every week.

As a young kid, I watched my mom go through a real emotional shift after the pastor left. She struggled with launching back into a working life. She took multiple jobs to make sure she wouldn't lose all the things she was now responsible for, such as the new house and her new furniture. As for the pastor's son, he ended up finishing high school with her help and went off to college with a Reserve Officers' Training Corps (ROTC) scholarship.

When the pastor walked out, there was a real vacuum in my mom's life. She had put her trust in him, and she was devastated. The man even left behind his own son! There she was, suddenly saddled with the extra responsibility of putting him through college plus all the bills. She likely felt guilty about any part she might have played in all this, bringing that man into her children's lives and whatnot. I think it all drove her into some kind of depression. But nothing kept her down for long.

My mom threw herself into work. Over the course of the next ten years, my mom often worked multiple jobs. She even became a licensed cosmetologist so she could do hair in the house. She was driving all the way to Savannah to take cosmetology classes at night. My mom opened a beauty salon, then another beauty salon, and when those didn't work out, she opened a day care.

Entrepreneurship was in the family, and nothing could take that away from her.

We always had food in the house. If I inherited one thing from my mom, it would be a strong work ethic and the guiding principle of doing whatever it takes. I never knew I had that within myself during the first eighteen years of my life because I had issues with self-confidence. But I later realized that seeing my mom work multiple jobs to make it all happen—to keep the lights on, keep food in the house, keep it together, raise five kids—was nothing short of amazing, and it gave me an internal road map for success later in life.

2

Pain is inevitable. Suffering is optional.
—Unknown

THE OVERWHELMING FEELING OF BEING different wasn't just due to my family's story. I believe a large part of the environment in which I grew up created some educational disadvantages. Hardeeville was like a lot of other southern towns. It was segregated back then, by choice—and that was after segregation was supposed to have ended. Today, previously all-White areas just twenty years ago are now more diverse due to a large influx of Hispanics working in the construction industry in nearby booming Hilton Head. It is a different community than the one I grew up in the 1980s and '90s.

After the Supreme Court decision in *Brown v. Board of Education*, schools were officially ordered to integrate. But one can't just stop decades or centuries of human behavior on a dime. Several private schools opened instead, and that's where the White families sent their children. You can find this scenario all over the South even today. Hardeeville itself was probably 60 percent White and 40 percent Black when I was growing up, with three private schools. The public school I went to seemed like it was 99.9 percent Black.

White families owned most of the businesses in Hardeeville. The same White families had owned the grocery store, newspaper, liquor store, gas stations, furniture store, and hardware store for generations. The idea of generational ownership of a cash-producing asset, like a business, was not common in the Black communities of the South that were dominated by segregationist polices. Parents of Black students often made an income barely above the poverty line. On a similar note, city lines were drawn to include a majority of White constituents, leaving most Black voters outside city lines. Consequently, Black votes had less influence, and that in turn determined the public services we received.

Taxes drove the school budget, so one can imagine the extent of the lack of funding in the public school system. In fact, the funding situation was so desperate that there was often only one school for multiple districts. Teachers were poorly paid, and there was a lot of turnover among the faculty. I certainly think this contributed to my lack of enthusiasm for academics. How could anyone get educated in such an environment?

There was a huge split between Whites and Blacks in Hardeeville, even though things were supposed to be equal on paper. The only time I ever interacted with White kids was when we played city sports. When I turned sixteen, that changed a little bit because I was hanging around the drug game crowd, so if any White kids wanted drugs, our paths might cross. But until then, it was just summer football. When the summer was over, we went our separate ways: the Black kids to public school and the White kids to private school. I recall that I went to a White friend's house *one* time for a birthday party. But other than that token event and summer football, we were completely separate.

Being located in the Deep South, even Hardeeville's cemeteries were separated by the road: White on one side and Black on the other. I remember one time, at the annual catfish festival, the Ku Klux Klan (KKK) marched in the parade. The owner of the liquor store was a former grand dragon, and we knew that KKK members owned certain stores. There wasn't necessarily any tension in terms of shopping at these stores, and many of them had Black employees. But even so, it was no secret these store owners were racist, and one could see it in some of the ways they acted, like calling grown Black employees "boy." On the other hand, there were some stores we just didn't go into, like the White barber or this one particular gas station.

I wasn't raised to think we were inferior, but there was always an awareness of the racial disparity between Whites and Blacks. There was a certain way to act and present ourselves around White people—and a certain way one might expect them to behave toward us. When I was in middle school, though I was technically too young to work, I ended up getting a job washing dishes at a steak house. One time, the owner came in and just threw thirty or forty metal salad pans at me and started yelling, but it was pretty typical of how he acted toward his Black staff. We all knew he looked down on us with some serious disdain.

When I was a sophomore and junior in high school, my aunt got me a job at a grocery store in Hilton Head, where she worked as a bookkeeper. I remember taking groceries out to cars that were worth $90,000 or maybe even $200,000. But I practically never saw that kind of wealth around people who looked like me, with the exception of carrying out groceries to Black folks taking a vacation. That kind of wealth just wasn't in my world, and I didn't understand how it was built. It didn't necessarily make me feel inferior, but it certainly raised questions. Why not us? Why not my mom? *Why not me?*

We used to get forms from Publishers Clearing House, and I would always push my mom to fill them out, just hoping we would win that kind of money. I never understood why we hadn't acquired the same wealth I saw in Hilton Head. I was fascinated by the economic disparity that existed in such close proximity. On either side of the Savannah Bridge, one could see Hilton Head or the Frazier housing projects.

It sunk in later in life that everyone doesn't start in the same place. But why doesn't everyone start in the same place? I believe—because I have seen—that equal access to quality education is not the same, and that is one of the most important factors leading to socioeconomic disparity.

This created a proverbial glass ceiling over my head: the dysfunctional family dynamic and the general socio-economic imbalance that existed for everyone who looked like me. Well into my adulthood, I carried the belief that there were only certain things that could and would be afforded to me. I never thought I would go to college or do anything other than just get a job and work. I believed that even if a person got a job, they didn't grow professionally. They just plateaued and lived a life of working to pay their bills. My childhood experiences only reinforced this notion.

Against this backdrop of social, economic, and educational inequality was the dysfunction of my family—namely, the strange relationship I had with my biological father. It's hard to describe the relationship I had with him. In some ways, I felt like a fatherless child. After the pastor left, my dad started coming around again. He would visit two days a week, mostly after work, which usually meant later at night. At that time, I had nothing else to compare our relationship against, other than those times when my siblings' father might take them fishing. Now that I have my own wife and kids, I can look back and say that my father and I did not have a normal, healthy relationship.

Hardeeville was actually a great place to grow up. It was a place where everyone knew each other. Even when I lived there in the nineties, anyone could have credit at the supermarket, and everyone looked out for each other. My favorite place was the neighborhood basketball court. We would hang out there all day. Until I was thirteen years old, it was pretty normal. We learned to hold our own, and we learned to settle conflicts with our fists. I was a very quiet kid, but a little taller and bigger than most my age, so I usually got the better end of most conflicts. They happened frequently.

If I ever needed anything from him, I had to leave a note on the dresser. We barely had any contact or conversation about what transpired. If I needed field trip money—say, six dollars—I wrote a note about it. If I got the money, it was on the note the next morning. If there was some sort of occasion for him, like a birthday, my mom would bring me a card to sign. Come Christmas and birthdays, I could almost guarantee I would get a gift from him. But that made the connection between us a transactional relationship. My dad never really took any interest in whatever I did in school. My mom would show him my report cards. But he never really got involved in my schoolwork, and he never came around to any of my football games during the summer. One time he took me to the fair, but it wasn't a fun memory—it was just awkward. How could I have a relationship with someone who only came around once or twice a week? Even spending time with him felt businesslike.

I would say I was a poor student, but I never felt dumb. I felt disengaged. I had an active imagination, and nobody held me accountable academically. Nobody was checking my homework or anything like that. I found my outlet was city league football. I started playing when I was six or seven, and I played for five years. There was the camaraderie of having friends, and there were great coaches, like my friend Devon's dad. His dad took an interest in helping me out, almost like he was a surrogate father. He picked me up from practice and brought me home. Come football trips, he helped me get to games or coordinated rides, and he made sure I ate.

Football created a supportive environment with a healthy challenge. I may not have cared so much about school, but I cared about football. Winning or losing meant so much, and the game was serious. We played full tackle back in those days. We were running laps and learning discipline. I think all that did give me something helpful for later in life when I joined the military. I learned how to shift into a mental state of putting my mind in a different place and pushing through a physical challenge. I found fulfillment in learning what I was made of and seeing how I could succeed at something. I believe team sports are critical to developing resiliency and social skills in adolescents. I was attracted to football because all the young boys in my town played football; it was the thing to do. I begged my mom to sign me up. Back then it was twenty-five dollars, which included all the equipment, so it was affordable. Initially, I did not like it. The coaches were volunteers, and they were tough. As I built my mental and physical stamina, I felt myself becoming tougher and more competitive.

When I failed the fourth grade, my mom told my dad, and he made her take me out of football. I remember the coaches pleading to let me play. They knew that football got me out of the house and gave me a sense of community, worth, and purpose. During that first summer without football, something changed in me. I really didn't care that I had failed in school. I wasn't playing football, which up until that point had been how I spent my summers. I was in a weird zone of isolation and loneliness. I didn't have a lot of friends in my neighborhood, because a lot of them were playing football. I became immersed in TV, as I had nothing else to do. I laid on the floor in my mom's room watching TV all day, a despondent eight- or nine-year-old. I never played football—or organized sports at all, for that matter—again. Football had been my outlet. I shifted into not caring about anything that might require some effort or responsibility.

I repeated the fourth grade during the following school year. Mrs. Webber was my teacher that year. She was the first teacher who seemed to truly care about my success, and she tried to hold me accountable. Our school system was among the worst in all of South Carolina, so getting a teacher who cared and was willing to invest effort into pushing her students toward success was a rarity. I started to excel in her class as a result. In fact, my second round of fourth grade was the first time I ever tried in school, all because of the way Mrs. Webber ran that classroom.

I remember getting good grades on the ten-question spelling test she used to give every week, and that became a source of pride for me. The way she handled our achievements by celebrating milestones made me *want* to do well. I felt like I was accomplishing something. Honestly, I wish I had followed up on that success because spelling has remained a challenge for me to this day.

Mrs. Webber was older and had received her teaching certification later in life. She wasn't in it for the money. She was from Hardeeville herself, so she knew the community, knew our parents, and knew the importance of getting an education. She was invested in the kids more so than her paycheck, and she showed a real passion for treating her students with dignity and respect. I still had a rage building inside me. I do not know where it came from, but I did not like anyone challenging me or making me feel lesser than. This truly was a defining moment. I remember one time I got in a fight outside her classroom. Two students confronted me in the hallway over a girl. At that point in my life, I was done being bullied, so I punched both of them in the face. The way she handled it was like she was disappointed in me, as if she had expected me to do better, which made me want to live up to her expectations. She made me feel like I could accomplish anything.

I did relatively well in middle school, and I think repeating the fourth grade with Mrs. Webber as my teacher helped me. I wasn't a star, but I cared enough because the teachers cared enough to pay attention to my academic performance. When I was in the sixth grade, they told me they were going to promote me to the eighth grade because they didn't see why I needed to be held back any longer. This meant I was catching right back up with the students who had been my classmates before we got to high school.

There was one particularly bright part of middle school for me. I met a teacher named Mrs. Thomas. She grew up in Hardeeville but had moved to New York and then came back to Hardeeville to teach and make a difference. So her perspective on education was a little bit different—and she was more invested—than most of the teachers around her. When I was in the sixth grade, she got me involved in an organization called STAR (Southern Teens Acting Responsibly). It was a small group, but we learned about positive principles and the value of community service. I believe this gave me the foundation of my activist spirit. My greatest memory in the organization is Ms. Thomas challenging the status quo to improve our community. She taught us not to sit on our hands and to be the change we wanted to see in our community. She took us to colleges, African American historical sites, and opened our minds. I believe she planted a seed in our minds even as some of us took different paths. We could change our communities from within. Although I could not see it then, today it is crystal clear what my responsibilities are in giving back.

STAR Community Engagement

I still wasn't playing sports, but I had a pretty good group of friends in my neighborhood. My mom was working a lot, and my siblings were often out of the house—as I mentioned, they were eight, nine, and even ten years older than me. By the time I was about ready to enter high school, my sisters had gotten married, my brother was married and had a family, and the preacher's son was going off to college and ROTC.

So it was just me in the house during those late middle school years. I learned some valuable skills about how to take care of myself. I would do my own laundry. My mom made sure there was food in the house, but I would fix myself something to eat since she was working. Sometimes friends who weren't as well off would come over, and I'd make something for them to eat, too. They were probably pretty impressed by our house because we also had some luxuries, like a dryer and a VCR, that my mom had worked hard to get. My mom worked really hard to keep things afloat. I knew we were not too bad off when I visited my friend's house. He lived in an older trailer that had plumbing issues. I enjoyed hanging out with him because he was just as curious as me. One day, I went into his refrigerator and saw a dead blackbird on a plate. I was shocked. I knew they did not have much, but I had never seen anyone eat a blackbird. I did not say anything. From that day on, I would always come over with extra food. It taught me a valuable lesson about life, opportunity, and perseverance. As I mentioned, even though I wasn't old enough to get a job, I got one anyway—washing dishes—making eighty to ninety dollars every two weeks and saving up the money. Unfortunately, this independence wasn't all good. I think it forced me to grow up a little too quickly. By the time I entered high school, I was street smart beyond my years, and I knew how the street game worked: I was primed and ready to get into trouble.

3

I don't believe in the no-win scenario.
—Captain Kirk

I ENTERED HIGH SCHOOL IN 1990. Since I had been bumped up into eighth grade, I was once again with my original class. I felt like I was back on track in terms of my education, but high school would prove to be an unexpected turning point.

Jasper County High School was a county high school about fifteen miles from where I lived. I was introduced to new people I had never met beyond the circle of friends I had grown up with on my street. With three different towns feeding into the same high school, there were a lot of rivalries between students from different places. Before high school, these were sports rivalries, but with the collision of students from various places, a lot of these rivalries became more serious. They took on tones of animosity, and there was definitely some tension between the different crowds. This was 1990, the height of the crack cocaine epidemic, and small-town America was not spared. By this time, I had already lost friends and relatives to prison, drug overdoses, and murder. My heightened sense of awareness was beyond any normal fourteen-year-old's.

When I entered the ninth grade, I wasn't paying attention to all that, though I did start widening my circle of friends. As far as the schoolwork part of high school went, I didn't really care. Even though I came into high school thinking it might be a fresh start, and I had even registered for college prep classes, I quickly fell into a pattern of not doing my homework, coming in late, and missing entire days of school. I wasn't trying to be disrespectful; I just didn't care.

I remember taking art as an elective course and sitting next to this one particular friend every day. One time he went to the bathroom, and the teacher, who had been searching for a lot of missing art supplies, went through my friend's bag and found a pistol. That friend got expelled, and even though I had nothing to do with it, that teacher looked at me differently for the rest of the year. I remember sitting there when he pulled the gun out of the bag and thinking, *Oh no, I'm going to be roped in on this.* And in a way, I was involved. The teacher failed me for that class. In his mind, I was connected with the gun. And because I had failed another class, I had to repeat ninth grade the following year.

To be honest, I didn't deserve to move on to the tenth

grade. I didn't care about the consequences of not receiving an education. The way the school system was set up facilitated such apathy. The guidance counselors didn't help students internalize the outcome of not planning for the future. They wouldn't tell students what was wrong with taking the easy math class instead of the hard math class because most students just wanted to get by instead of challenging themselves. I put some effort into my English class because the teacher was a longtime friend of my mom's. I wasn't afraid she would tell my mom about my academic performance. Rather, it was because I had a more personal connection. I knew she cared and that she really wanted us to learn.

I don't think I can say I learned anything academic in the ninth grade. I had no desire to be in class. I had an after-school job I went to here and there at the steak house. Fourteen or fifteen years old at the time, I felt like I had already settled into the rest of my life, which was a ridiculous sentiment. But that's just the kind of climate the educational system was fostering: hopelessness. What I knew then was that I was going to work in the service industry, just like my mom and dad and everyone else in Hardeeville who looked like me. I was probably going to get involved in the drug game. Many of my friends had already served time in a juvenile prison. I was one of the few who wasn't getting officer visits at school or taking a visit to juvie. I think I have to credit my mom for keeping me somewhat on the straight and narrow. Despite the apathy I had about school, college, and my future, I did have a healthy dose of fear and respect for her—and my aunt Thelma, who kept good tabs on me.

I did things behind their backs, but I would only go so far. Even though I knew a lot of people who had dropped out of school to sell drugs—even in middle school—I didn't get into drug dealing as a career choice. But I still dabbled in marijuana. I had no healthy outlet like sports. I was just hanging out, and that led to doing the wrong kind of activities. I remember we would drink alcohol and not even really try to hide it. Since I had a car, I was kind of looked up to as a leader. Even though it was pretty dilapidated, it got us around. Looking back on it all, I was really lucky. I was doing things that could've landed me in juvie, but because of my mom, my aunt, and a brother-in-law I admired, I tried to run straight as best as I could.

Somehow I got enough credits during the first semester of my repeated ninth grade year to get bumped into the tenth grade. But that year things kind of conspired to keep me from doing well in school. When I was in the ninth grade, I had cousins who were seniors, so I ended up under their wing. Their presence had shielded me from territorial battles. But once they had graduated, things completely changed.

A lot of disputes would start over talking to girls. Everybody had grown up in their own towns with the same group of girls. With three different towns feeding into Jasper County High School, everybody was trying to talk to girls they had never met, which led to some problems. I had avoided that drama during ninth grade, but it caught up with me in the tenth grade. My involvement with alcohol and marijuana increased. I was around drug sales every day, and I saw a lot of people go to jail. I saw cops routinely coming to school to arrest students for crimes they had committed after school. Some of the teachers cared, and others turned a blind eye. This was all just the new normal for me.

I have to say, I did have some teachers who really stood out. I had a great English teacher one year, an awesome geography teacher, and a French teacher who really cared. But most of their colleagues weren't as invested. I couldn't blame them. They were underpaid, the school was understaffed, and the faculty was trying to teach a majority student population that had high pregnancy rates, high dropout rates, and came from low-income households—the children of folks just trying to make it happen with not a whole lot of extra time or money to reach for a better future.

All this created a huge challenge for the teachers to get students motivated about doing math, learning history, or memorizing the periodic table of elements. For most of us, the greatest achievement would be graduating high school. I had a lot of friends drop out because they knew the outcome of their high school diploma would just be getting a service industry job. What did that piece of paper matter if that was as good as it was going to get?

My mind was plugged into this belief my first two years of high school. There wasn't much at home pushing me out of this mindset, either. My mom was still working out of the home a lot. My dad was basically out of the picture. I had an after-school job that was giving me money. I had cousins and friends in the drug game, and they were always needing to get around. Since I had a car, they might give me a little bit of money to take them to different places, like if they needed to meet up with a connection.

I wasn't selling anything myself, because I had family connections that allowed me to refrain from needing to be a full-fledged drug dealer. But I was getting a street education and learning about the hustle. It was all about making things happen. But it wasn't the hustle of working hard forty hours a week or getting a proper education. It was more about getting an advantage or an edge on things so one could stay on top in a lifestyle that was all about fast money.

I wasn't paying much attention to math in school, but I sure learned about trap math, like how to size up large stacks of bills and count money quickly. I saw large exchanges of cash a lot, and that was just part of the drug game. I remember the first time I saw crack cocaine being cooked. I thought, *These are some smart people. What if they were able to use all this knowledge legitimately? They may be CEOs of a Fortune 500 company. What do they have that we do not have?* It was all about the fast life, and sometimes a fast life meant a quick death. I saw the back end of the excitement as well—consequences like a drug overdose or jail time. It was during this time I saw the consequences up close and personal. My cousin received an eighteen-year sentence for less than $200 of crack cocaine in his possession. He was seventeen years old.

My tenth-grade performance was even worse than ninth grade in terms of academics. I didn't even know my high school locker combo. It was just about getting to school and making it through the day, the week, the month, the year. I could've held a record for the most tardies. I was just existing. Some of the older kids in my group had graduated, so I became the de facto leader. I guess having a car helped make that happen. But that wasn't a role I wanted to fulfill. I remember one day the vice principal called me in and called me a *gang leader*, which totally threw me off. We didn't have gangs in Hardeeville.

There were some things we would do that may have given the impression of us being a gang. There was this fashion to wear white shirts and fisherman vests at the time. We used to do stuff like wear each other's vests —trading them out, as we called it—but that wasn't supposed to be a gang statement. At the same time, we were tight-knit and certainly involved in some of the things I mentioned—the drugs, the alcohol, and the territorial beefs. And that was becoming my identity. People saw me as a drug dealer even though I wasn't actually selling any drugs. We weren't criminals. We were just surviving our environment.

When I was in the eleventh grade, I still had one older cousin who was around. He was quickly becoming one of the biggest drug dealers in our area, and I was hanging out with him a lot, almost daily. He was taking care of me financially. I'd come into school with nice clothes and nice sneakers. At this point I was on my third car. I was a junior in high school who had no parental involvement in my car payments. Owning a car was a huge feat for someone who worked a few hours a week, but that was where the hustle part came in.

This cousin became a drug dealer known for moving

weight. I was still drinking during the week. Of course, we were drinking on the weekends as well with adults we knew. I had no outlook on what I was going to do after high school. My grades were poor. My grade point average (GPA) was barely high enough to graduate. I was pretty much just going through the motions and nothing more.

There was a really good friend of mine who was a senior and was going to join the marines after high school. One night we were driving around joyriding like we used to do. We picked up another guy who had been in and out of school due to a few stints in jail. When we picked him up, I found out he was looking for someone who owed him money—which probably explained why he was carrying—which led to everything that happened next.

We went to a local restaurant—no big deal—where we knew most of the girls behind the counter. The friend we picked up showed them a pistol, and then we left. He asked me to drop him off in the projects. Once we were there, we got flagged down by an older gentleman who said the police were looking for us because we had attempted to rob the restaurant at gunpoint. I guess the police were doing sweeps all around the neighborhood, and the word was out: we were wanted. He knew my car, so he flagged us down to let us know the cops were actively searching for us.

With that kind of news, my friend wanted to collect some clothes and belongings from the projects and then go to another friend's house to lay low for a while. As we exited the projects and took a left toward the place he was going, there was a patrol car on the side of the road. It had to be one of the cop cars looking for us—and it was. As they saw us pull out of the projects, they got behind my car and turned on their lights. My house happened to be in the same direction we were going, and I was a mile away from home, so I made the decision that I was going to make it to my yard and see what would happen from there.

Of course, when I pulled into my driveway, the cops jumped out. They surrounded the car and took us out at gunpoint. Suddenly, I was on the ground. My friend with the pistol took off running, and although the cops didn't catch him then, they caught up to him hiding behind a house him a few hours later. My mom was screaming outside our house.

At that moment, I realized that everything I thought I was headed toward was now happening. I hadn't really given the consequences much thought, but now I was seeing it all in real time. Bad things had happened to people I knew. I knew people who went to juvenile hall. I knew others who were killed stealing cars or in bad drug deals. And now it was my turn. It felt like that moment was my initiation into that world. This was it: I was going to go to prison over this.

The cops handcuffed us, picked us up off the ground, and searched my car, where they found my friend's pistol in the back seat—fully loaded. That friend went to prison for eight or nine years over that. I didn't get charged with anything. They learned that our visit to the restaurant wasn't actually an armed robbery, but his past record and a weapons charge put him in jail. My other friend did end up going into the marine corps, but it's crazy how close that opportunity came to being taken away from him.

That was my wake-up moment. Up until that day, I took things in stride. Up until that day, I figured my destiny was sealed. I knew being around drugs and drug sales and illegal activity was just going to be my life. I had been consciously choosing to do whatever I wanted, regardless of the consequences.

That summer, I did some soul-searching.

So, I entered my senior year of high school. Even after that wake-up call, I still took school just as seriously as I had taken grades nine, ten, and eleven. Despite my total apathy, there was a system in place to move kids through high school. I didn't deserve the grades I received. With most of my classes, the teacher just passed me. Even if I didn't turn in anything, I was good for a C. Once I figured that out, I didn't care. I had a loyal group of friends, and now I was on my fourth vehicle—a money-green Jeep decked out in chrome. I was seventeen years old, with thousands of dollars in my pocket, and a closet full of clothes. I was partying like a rock star at the after-hours spots. We were young and crazy, and even some of the adults looked up to us.

I was still looked at as the ringleader, but we weren't getting into serious trouble. We thought our hustle was airtight. For the most part, this was true. But there was still trouble. I remember one night we were hanging out in the projects at a friend's house, and a young man from another town came to visit his girlfriend. Since we had some rivalries between the different areas, he really shouldn't have been there. To teach him a lesson, some folks, including some of my friends, got the bright idea to vandalize his car. They tore it up, broke the windows, and started beating on the door of his girlfriend's house, trying to get him to come out.

There was always going to be a fight if anyone ventured into the wrong part of town, or worse if they came across the wrong group of people—there was no getting out of it. When we were brave or stupid enough to go to clubs in other areas, it was almost guaranteed that there was going to be a shoot-out. That was just the nature of the beast. Since my money-green Jeep with chrome trim was in the projects that night—and it was pretty hard to miss—he assumed I was part of the group who had smashed up his car. It didn't help that I was kind of looked at as the de facto leader of the group.

When I got to school the next morning, there was a large group of about twenty people waiting for me. I didn't think anything of it at first. Some of them were even friends I had made from different towns when I was in the ninth grade and before I got brought into all this craziness. But because they had relatives from the same place as the kid whose car got wrecked that night, they were now against me. Of course, those friendships fell off and haven't been repaired to this day.

The mob was spread out on either side of the hallway. As I started walking to class, they taunted me, trying to get me to fight. At this point I was not interested in fighting. Most of the people I hung around with after school were well-established hustlers, and fighting did not make money. Then, I saw the guy whose car had been totaled.

I knew what they were after. I started thinking about how I could defend myself. I figured I just had to get to my science class. Maybe I could make my own version of Custer's Last Stand.

Of the twenty or so students who had been waiting in the hall, around seven or so followed me into the science classroom. They moved in to take me down, so I pushed some of the desks away and grabbed a protractor with a sharp tip. If the teacher didn't come in, I was ready to defend myself. I remember thinking, *I just bought this outfit.* I had on an outfit that cost approximately $500, and I was not about to allow it to get messed up. I knew someone who had gotten their ribs cracked during a confrontation, and I knew that wasn't going to be me. At the very least, I wasn't going to let it happen easily. As it turned out, the teacher came in and diffused the situation. Nothing really happened that day, but it was typical of the serious feuding that was going on all the time.

During the second semester of my senior year, some of my friends got expelled for various things. At one point the administration said they thought it would be best if I didn't come back for a few days. I said whatever to that and decided I wouldn't come back at all. I was just four or five months from graduating, and I was only supposed to be gone for a week. But a week turned into two weeks, and that turned into a month. I had made a decision to enlist in the air force after high school, but that wasn't going to happen if I didn't graduate. I believed the door was opening for me to do something better, but years of apathy and bad habits were pushing back. I knew I had only a few options. Once I decided on the military, I knew I had to do everything to make it happen. I had a running list of how I would tackle it: try the air force, then the army, then the marines, then the navy. If military service did not work out, I was actually considering joining the peace corps. Basically, my plan included any option that would allow me to escape my situation. Thankfully, my French teacher stepped in and sent a message to me through a younger female cousin. She had talked to the other teachers and tried to figure out how to help make sure I graduated. I didn't turn in anything those last few months of high school. In fact, I didn't even show up. But they gave me the grades I needed to pass.

Part of being around people in the drug game helped me see how crazy it could get outside high school. I was apathetic about academics—and life in general—but I saw how hopeless things could get. Hardeeville, like many places, was hit hard by the crack epidemic during the 1980s. I remember we used to light a bonfire and hang out. There was a guy we called Junior who would come around, and he had been a crack addict for years. He'd do chores like cut grass for money, and, of course, he'd use that money for drugs.

One time he came around to the bonfire looking for money or crack or anything he could trade to get his fix. Someone said, "Pick up that hot log," and he was ready to follow through. I watched this man stick his arm into a raging fire and pick up a red-hot log with his bare hand. I can still hear his skin sizzling. His hand had severe burns on it—all for ten dollars to get a fix. Lessons like this showed me what someone would be willing to do for drugs—what hopelessness really looked like. The power of having *no control* over yourself. Things like that pushed me to find a way out of all this—to change my mindset and change my identity. I thought that if I didn't, I might turn into Junior.

In my last year of high school, I developed insomnia. I would come home and stay up until the sun came out and then just go back to functioning the next day. The stress of thinking someone was coming for me—that certain people were against me—kept me up all night. It was not uncommon to have people you grew up with plot to rob you. It was a crazy time, and you could not really trust anyone. It was not like I was depositing large sums of cash into the bank. No. People knew or assumed you always had something of value. I was a flashy dresser and wore a very large Gucci link gold chain with a medallion of Elmer Fudd holding a shotgun. I was a walking target. The anxiety of getting trapped in Hardeeville prevented me from sleeping. I was doing so much self-reflection until six or seven in the morning. I developed a little bit of paranoia, and I was constantly looking out the window because I had one or two friends whose homes got shot up. Then, of course, there was all the stuff that had actually happened to me, like the incident at the restaurant and the car. I started developing this visualization against my will that someone was going to kill me. I knew that I had to leave Hardeeville. I just didn't know how.

4

Life begins at the end of your comfort zone.
—Neale Donald Walsh

I ENTERED MY SENIOR YEAR of high school in the fall of 1993. I had no idea what I was going to do after graduation. I didn't have the SAT scores to go to college. My *combined* score was below seven hundred, which didn't even meet the minimum requirement for most colleges, and my GPA hovered between a two and a three. My peers who were going to college were mostly going to an open enrollment college like Denmark Technical College, a local community outfit. If they had performed better academically, they might be going to a historically Black college or university. But there were also plenty of kids who had dropped out to get in the drug game or for other reasons. As for me, I had no idea how I would get into college or how I would pay for it. College was like something I couldn't afford and shouldn't bother to think about. Some of my friends who were going off to college were paying for it with a sports scholarship, but I hadn't played any sports since being taken out of summer football after fourth grade. Despite all that, I still filled out the applications because it seemed like the right thing to do. Like most other things concerning school, I just went through the motions.

Even with all this uncertainty, I knew I had to do something. The soul-searching I had done that summer led me to think I definitely did not want to get trapped in the drug game or in prison. At the same time, I had no ambition or academic ability to go to college. I think I was resigned to the idea of settling into a service industry job, but I was concerned trouble would catch up with me as it had for so many others.

I was walking down the hallway at school when I saw the air force recruiter. His blue uniform threw me off a little bit because the air force didn't really recruit at my high school. I was intrigued. We got into a little bit of a conversation, and he asked my name. His name was Todd as well. He looked up my Armed Services Vocational Aptitude Battery (ASVAB) scores right there on the spot in a binder he had with him, and he gave me the bad news. "I don't think you meet the qualifications for the air force. Maybe you need to look at a different service."

I had taken the ASVAB in the tenth grade, just like everyone else who had wanted to get out of class, but I hadn't taken it seriously. So that was the end of the conversation. A few days went by, but something about him turning me away intrigued me. Plus, it also sounded cool: *the air force.* I opened the yellow pages and looked up where I might find him. The nearest air force recruiting station was in Beaufort, roughly thirty minutes away. I drove there and went to his office unannounced.

Hardeeville was located in what many called an army region, and I had tons of relatives in the army. While the air force didn't recruit much in my high school, there were usually at least four army recruiters hounding students to join—and many of them did because it was viewed as a decent way out of a trouble-filled lifestyle. Military bases abounded in the area, like the marine corps station at Parris Island (thirty minutes away), Savannah's Hunter Army Airfield (fifteen minutes away), and Fort Stewart (forty-five minutes away). But despite the military presence, I never saw anyone in an air force uniform. That's why his blue uniform caught my attention.

The recruiting office in Beaufort was in a strip mall with a Taco Bell and a grocery store. It was a small office with recruiters from all different branches of the service—navy, army, marines, and the air force. There were two desks in his office—one for another recruiter I hadn't met. In the waiting room, he showed me some VHS tapes presenting different air force career options.

He didn't remember me that first time I came to his office. I reminded him that we had talked in the hallway of Jasper County High School, that I told him I was interested in learning more about the air force, and that he suggested I look at some other services because of my ASVAB scores. I think driving all the way out to Beaufort spoke to him. He asked me what my name was,

I reminded him, and then he remembered me.

He looked up my score again, and he reiterated that my score was below the minimum criteria to enlist in the air force. But this time it wasn't the end of the conversation. He asked about when I had taken the test, and I told him I had taken it two years ago. He said people usually get at least the minimum score, and he asked if I felt like I had it in me to retake the test.

The military was the number one escape route where I was from, but I didn't know anyone in the air force. My cousins and relatives went into the army. The ASVAB scores to get into the air force needed to be higher, so the low academic achievement in our schools didn't facilitate that. And the air force recruiters knew that, so they didn't bother coming around. But this recruiter was willing to give me another chance. He asked if I was serious, and I said yes. I wanted that opportunity. He set up another test, he took me to the testing location, and I took the exam.

I was nervous taking the test. I didn't think I was going to pass. A lot of people I knew who had taken the ASVAB hadn't scored well enough to get into the air force, and I assumed they were smarter than me. They appeared to be going to class, paying attention, doing their homework—and I wasn't doing any of that. So why would I pass a test they couldn't?

But the recruiter gave me some study materials. There was math, mechanics, aviation questions, and some word associations. While I always felt stronger about the English part, the math part was not my strong suit. I know I didn't score well on that part.

The recruiter waited outside the door while I took the test. I think he definitely wanted me to succeed. A week later, he called and said he had some good news. I had made the minimum requirement, but just barely. He said he could potentially find some jobs I would qualify for in the air force, and we started talking about those positions. I was relieved about passing. Truth be told, if I hadn't passed, I probably would've entered some other branch of the service after high school.

I didn't tell a single person in my family what was happening. I was seventeen years old, and I couldn't sign the paperwork until I turned eighteen on February 10. For a few months, I went to meet the recruiter every two weeks to talk about the air force while he just held on to my paperwork. The Delayed Enlistment Program (DEP) for new recruits involved coming back to the recruiter for some light drilling, talking about air force culture, and providing general tips, but only after a recruit had signed the paperwork. My recruiter allowed me to come back to the office on Saturdays and participate in the DEP even though I hadn't signed up yet. I also had an opportunity to talk with some recruits who had just finished basic military training (BMT) and to meet kids from different areas.

It was also comforting to have an adult in my life who cared about me and could communicate realistic opportunities for me. I was intrigued by his professionalism, and I aspired to be like him. The recruiter wanted to call my parents and get them involved because I couldn't sign, but I didn't want to involve anyone. When my birthday finally came, I signed up for the enlistment program, and he filed the paperwork.

I was only eligible for a few jobs. I wanted to be a firefighter, but I didn't meet qualifications on high-pitch hearing. The next occupation on my list was something administrative. I was going to be a medical records technician. That was my guaranteed job. Once I signed the paperwork, we kept in touch. He didn't have a date yet for me to ship out to basic training, but he told me all I needed to do at this point was graduate high school.

I never told my recruiter about the huge feud I was involved in over the car that had gotten smashed up in the projects. And when the fallout from all that reached a point of me needing to leave high school, I didn't tell him that I thought about not coming back. I was mentally done. I was not sleeping, I was drinking heavily, and I became more and more paranoid and numb. I started increasing my appetite for dangerous behavior. I now owned a firearm, and I gave up on any possible future. If I had, he probably would've taken me out of the program, I wouldn't have gone into the air force, and my life would've been completely different. Thankfully, at that point the French teacher stepped in and arranged for me to pass even though I never showed up, except to walk at graduation.

I eventually told my parents about what was happening, though I didn't tell them until April. Even after I passed the ASVAB and I knew that I would be heading off to the air force, I didn't tell anyone. It finally came out during a family blowup. I received a letter notifying me I had been rejected by Georgia Southern University. It was no surprise to me. In fact, I had forgotten I applied. I only applied because some friends did, but my dad was furious when my mom showed him the letter.

He came at me with a salvo of questions about what I was going to do with my life, talking about how he wasn't going to pay for me to go to technical college, which was weird to me because in all those years of high school he had never really shown so much as a care for how I did in school or otherwise. I think he was happy he wouldn't have to pay for me to go anywhere. I think he had a bad impression of me. He had some side businesses that he had never let me work for, like his window washing and carpet cleaning businesses. He thought I would mess it up. So, when he started yelling and going on, I blurted out, "I joined the air force." It got real quiet.

He didn't know what to say, and for some reason we spoke even less after that night. We barely spoke until I left for BMT, except for one time when he went out of his way to tell me he heard I was the local weed man. I didn't bother to respond to that.

I made it through high school and got my diploma. It was the summer of 1994. The recruiter called me and said he had a few tentative dates for me to ship out to basic training: December 1994 or January 1995. That meant I had six or seven months before BMT. During this time, I wasn't working. I just hung out with the folks I knew in the drug game. I wasn't trying to get into any trouble; I was trying to keep a low profile. I had just come off people trying to harm me. I had insomnia and couldn't sleep at night. I would only go outside the neighborhood with my cousin or people who I knew had my back. I wouldn't go out to clubs, because the few times I did, there were weapons involved or a shoot-out or people plotting to harm me.

Fast-forward to September, when I left for BMT. My dad did come out to give me a ride to the airport with my mom. The last thing he said to me that day was that he thought I'd be back home in two weeks. Well, twenty-five years, seven months, and seventeen days later, I retired from the air force with the highest enlisted rank. And in all that time, he never attended one ceremony.

The recruiter had me come to his office every two weeks to go over expectations. To drive to Beaufort, I had to drive through two communities where the people didn't care for me. Even though I had just turned eighteen, I did a lot of fishing, so I had a legal .22 long rifle with a short barrel and a pistol grip. I always had it in my Jeep because I felt like I wouldn't be safe if someone who didn't like me caught me.

One day, I was coming back home from my DEP meeting with the recruiter. I was stopped at a traffic light and saw a guy who I knew disliked me. I had heard that if he ever caught me, he was going to harm me. He made a U-turn to roll up next to me and stopped. I had a decision to make: Was I going to stop and engage, or drive away? My pride wanted me to get out. But I also knew that if I got out with a weapon, my life would be taking a different turn. As I looked down at that rifle, I knew if I engaged with him, he would harm me, or I would harm him.

I drove away from the situation and headed back home.

Don't get me wrong: I was still getting into trouble. Wherever I was, even if I tried to avoid it, trouble found me. One day, the recruiter called me and said I could leave for basic training early. I said great—I needed to go. He told me if I kept out of trouble I could leave in September, and he was going to get me to the Military Entrance Processing Stations (MEPS). I passed everything at the MEPS, and at that point I was just waiting.

This was a time of significant change in my life. I spent most of my teenage years in a poorly structured environment. I didn't follow any rules, and I lived by a code that placed a heavy price on trust and loyalty.

On September 14, 1994, I got on my first airplane ride to Texas. I was eighteen, and this was the first time I was completely out of my comfort zone. I can remember the unfamiliar sights and sounds of walking through the airport. All these years and hundreds of airports later, those memories of how I felt taking off, landing, and the sound of the engine on my way to BMT still resonate with me. But above all, BMT was the first time in my life I understood that I was capable of learning something if I put my mind to it.

With everything I had experienced growing up, I wasn't afraid of people yelling at me or the physical work of BMT. When we arrived in Texas, we boarded an old city bus to transport us to Lackland Air Force Base in San Antonio. The first thing they did was line us up on some footprints, and they started yelling at us. They put us into bays of about fifty trainees, and I remember hearing some crying that night—probably some people wondering what they had gotten themselves into. This entire scene was unfamiliar. I was a young Black man with limited life skills. The first night they told us all to take a shower and shave. At this point in my life, I had never used a razor to shave, and I had no clue what to do. I had cuts all over my face. Taking a shower with thirty other men was also a new experience. I think the initial shock of it all made me buckle down into a shell to prepare myself to get through it.

BMT went pretty quickly. We would get up early; get dressed; do some PT (exercise); go to different classes; and then spend the afternoon drilling, marching, and learning ceremony. We were assigned jobs in basic training. During BMT, there's a senior flight that takes care of new recruits and shows them the ropes. I was told the two jobs everyone would try to get were being a chapel guide and being on laundry crew. Laundry crew got new recruits out of getting yelled at, as they were away in the laundry room. Chapel gave new recruits an opportunity to go to church and spend their entire Sunday away from the barracks and all the yelling. I thought that sounded good, so I became a chapel guide helping out at religious services.

I was assigned a bunkmate during BMT—a wingman to help with day-to-day responsibilities. My bunkmate was a short guy from Ohio. I would say that I still had an independent streak in me during BMT, and I was still learning to develop my team-player skills. In fact, at least once I was threatened with being recycled—that is, being returned to day one of BMT. I was even told to pack up my bags. I feel like there was some tension between Blacks and Whites in the air force, and me keeping to myself gave the element leaders something to complain about.

My bunkmate and I did not get along. With all the stress going on, there was sure to be hostility between people, so an altercation was not totally outside the realm of possibility. Despite the fact that we didn't get along, I always tried to do everything right on my end. One day, I asked him to help someone else out with something, and he jumped in my face, telling me he wasn't going to be nobody's punk. So, I started to cuss him out. He told me if I talked to him like that where he was from, I would disappear. This was the first racial incident I had experienced in the air force. Even coming from a small southern town, I had never experienced such an overt threat. I think I was naive in thinking this did not occur in the military. I was so wrong. The military is a microcosm of society, and I would continue to learn these life lessons.

I'll never forget those words because I wanted to choke him right then and there. Our element leader, a fellow in charge of roughly thirteen individuals, happened to witness the exchange. He was the only Black element leader in our flight, so I think he knew how to diffuse the situation. He pulled me back, and it's a good thing he did because I was about to fight. That was my first racial incident in the air force. I had thought things like that wouldn't happen in the military, but I was wrong. A few years later, I got even with that bunkmate.

They gave me a booklet of general air force knowledge. I studied it every day because we had to carry it with us all the time. I think I overstudied because of my academic fears. As soon as they told me I was taking a test on the material, my fears went into overdrive. Everyone took a test on the material in the booklet at the end of BMT, which totaled around six weeks. I placed the highest of anyone, with a score of ninety-six. I remember everyone was in one room when they announced the scores, and I couldn't believe it. It was a bit validating because I had problems with some of the element leaders and the dorm chief. There were study sessions at night, and I would skip out on them because I didn't think they were productive. I would go back to my bed and study by myself, which the leadership didn't like. They thought I wasn't being a team player. So, when I got that high score, it was vindicating. The other people in my flight looked like they were in disbelief.

I had never achieved anything like that academically. I realized something: I could learn anything just by looking at the same information hundreds of times until I internalized it. That was my method of learning. Learning is about having confidence, and during this time I had little to no confidence in my ability to learn. I can say this moment was a huge turning point in my life—one that would lead me to face my education deficiencies head-on.

In the last week of BMT, they handed out jobs. I was expecting to be a hospital records technician. But they gave me my folder, and it read "security police." I was baffled. I raised my hand and told the gentleman handing out assignments that he made a mistake. He said I needed to speak to a technician if there was an error.

It was at this point that I unraveled what had happened. I was supposed to leave for basic training in December or January, but I had gotten to leave earlier because my mom had been calling the air force recruiter over and over again, saying that I was getting in trouble and that they had to get me out of Hardeeville. My recruiter made it happen, but that meant I had to enter the air force as what's called open general, meaning they would assign me a role after BMT.

I had no idea that this had happened. So here I was, arguing with the technician. But once that all came out, I had no choice but to accept the job they gave me, which was essentially being a police officer for the military.

My older brother had gone into law enforcement, but I didn't want to do that. Up until that point, I never had any positive interactions with law enforcement. It wasn't that I didn't respect the police. I just had no desire to become a police officer, even in the military. At eighteen years old, this was my worst nightmare, but I knew I had to take this job to remain in the air force. I remember the walk back into the massive room where everyone was sitting. People were happy to be moving on from BMT, but I was absolutely down with my prospects of where I was headed. A cop? Really? My recent memories with law enforcement consisted of being profiled during traffic stops, which built up uneasiness due to my own activities.

I started law enforcement training at the same base I had gone through BMT: Lackland Air Force Base. I was a little disappointed as I watched other recruits get shipped off to more exciting places. To my surprise, though, I found that I loved the police training. I fell in love not with policing but with the leadership aspect. It was the first time I got put in charge of my flight, and I excelled. I was completely surprised by how intrigued and interested I became with the law. They taught us about law, the Uniform Code of Military Justice (UCMJ), and how to respond to incidents. They even taught us how to direct traffic. They taught us everything a regular law enforcement officer would learn, and I actually found it exciting. Being elevated to that leadership role—getting put in charge of forty-five people—showed me that I had some inherent leadership skills. I started developing the *Why not me?* mindset.

All this military training was the first time I succeeded on both physical and mental fronts. I graduated pretty high in the class and as a student leader. BMT helped me realize I could learn and succeed if I put my mind to it. Law enforcement training was the first time I realized I was capable of doing something above average. Air base ground defense training came next, at Fort Dix, New Jersey. I graduated technical training before Christmas.

As it turned out, it was good that my mom had hounded the recruiter about getting me shipped out as early as possible. During the first week of BMT, they let recruits make a call home. During that call, my mom told me the cousin I hung around with had been stopped by the cops. He had drugs in the car, fled the state, and was on the run. I knew without a shadow of a doubt that if I had not left for BMT I would've been in that car—probably driving that car—and I would've been arrested or gone on the run myself. That was chilling. My mom may have saved my entire life and my career. If I had been pulled over with him, I would've had to decide whether to run or to get charged for crimes—and neither would have led to a life I wanted.

After training, we were told we could go home for ten days for the Christmas holiday. By then I had been through BMT and law enforcement training. Even though this process only spanned five to six months, I was a completely different person. I'll never forget getting picked up from the airport in full service dress. I remember walking into my mom's house. She used to have folks there all the time. My great-grandmother had moved in after suffering a stroke while I was in high school. When I stepped into her home, I felt like I was walking through a sea of people in my uniform, all decked out, people saying congratulations. At the same time, I felt out of place. Those early years chipped away at any self-confidence I had, and I had a hard time accepting positive feedback, which I have struggled with throughout my adult life.

I remember that night a friend called and asked if I wanted to go out to a club in Hilton Head. Something felt odd about going out. I was a different person now. So I said no thanks. Fast-forward to three o'clock that morning. I got another call. My friend had been killed. He was with the group of guys I would've gone out with that night. I had looked up to him. He graduated a year before me and had gone to junior college on a basketball scholarship. I remember picking him up to carpool to school in the mornings. We had double-dated for prom. That night, he had been shot and killed. I'll never forget that night. I had a panic attack. How many times had I come *this close* to my life being so different? It got me asking questions: *Why have I done so many things to run the wrong way, and I still keep getting saved?* Growing up and seeing wealth around me, but never with people who looked like me, I had asked, *Why not me?* Now I was reflecting on those close calls and asking myself the flip side of the same question: *Why me?*

5

Don't let others decide who you are.
—Dennis Rodman

ON FEBRUARY 10, 1995—MY BIRTHDAY—I was done with all my training. I had finished BMT, technical school, and air base ground defense training one year after I had signed the paperwork to enlist in the air force. I had received my badge and my beret, and I was a full-fledged police officer in the military. I was on my way to Maxwell Air Force Base in Alabama for my first duty assignment at Air University, the main campus for the educational arm of the air force.

I was excited to get to my first assignment after months of training. Things had been great at Fort Dix, with no real issues. In tech training, they asked us where we wanted to go by filling out something called the dream sheet. The way I was raised, the idea of going too far away from home wasn't common. After all, most people stuck around and worked in Hilton Head. But at the same time, I had looked through those encyclopedias as a young kid and saw all sorts of exciting far-off places.

I had a little bit of internal conflict about where I wanted to be assigned. I actually had orders to ship out to Nellis Air Force Base near Las Vegas. But Nevada seemed too far away from home, even though *home* was something I felt like I had just narrowly escaped. So I traded Nellis for Maxwell, just outside of Montgomery, Alabama, which was only five hours away from Hardeeville. Deep inside, I was still that unsure kid with no self-confidence. I was afraid to be far away from the environment that still dominated most of my thoughts. Years later I did end up going to Las Vegas, and I thought, *Wow, I could've been living here.* But at the time, I still needed something more familiar.

When I got to Maxwell, I started working the gates, which was a common assignment for new police officers. I liked it. I allowed all the vehicles to come through, checked the tags, the people, and made sure their authorizations were up to date. It was my nineteenth birthday, and I had this great sense of responsibility about my job. Pretty soon after that, they started a special gate section: ambassador elite. I was not looking to be singled out, but I was tall, slim, and looked good in uniform. I initially resisted the opportunity because I was still unsure of my abilities and did not want to fail. I soon accepted the opportunity and enjoyed the quick notoriety that came along with it. I got to wear a special tailored uniform, enjoy free dry cleaning, and I worked six-hour shifts while everyone else worked eight. I was the first person anyone would see when they came on base, so I had to have a top-notch appearance. Out of 140 security personnel, only 20 were selected. I was so proud to be on that gate section. Despite all that excitement and energy about starting my duty assignment, I was about to get taken down a notch.

It was at Maxwell that I experienced my second bout of racism in the military. The first one was the comment my bunkmate made during basic training—that someone like me wouldn't dare to talk back to someone like him in his hometown. This time around, it wasn't a comment made to my face, but in many ways it was a lot more damaging because it put me on edge and brought back some of the paranoia I endured during my last year of high school.

My supervisor was about eight years older than me, and he was White. He picked me up when I arrived and seemed to be genuinely concerned about ensuring an easy transition into the squadron. There were a few Black airmen I had seen around me, but not too many. I didn't feel much racial tension at this point. There was nothing overtly racist about anyone around me. Almost three months into my duty assignment, I heard some comments that cued me into an undercurrent that wasn't so visible.

There was this six-foot mirror outside the break room. This mirror had some inspiring words on it and a picture of what we should look like—sharp and proud. We used to spend hours working on our uniforms, shining our boots, and making sure our gloves were clean.

One day, I was adjusting my uniform in front of this mirror. I heard three voices in the break room. A conversation was going on inside. One of them was my direct supervisor, and the other two were E4 senior airmen—all of them were White males. They were talking about a few different things before the conversation turned toward the few Black airmen—one of them actually female. One of them said he felt sorry for my supervisor because he had to supervise all three Blacks on the flight. He started talking about the attitude one of the other Black airmen had and how if he were in charge of us, he would kick us *all* out. Another guy talked about his goal to sleep with the female Black airman. Within six months, the other black male on my flight was separated from the air force for a series of infractions that seemed minor to me. It felt like he was targeted because of how he carried himself.

It was eye-opening and shocking. My direct supervisor was always polite and cordial to me in person. To be fair, he was doing more listening to these two than talking, but what upset me was that he didn't refute their words or tell them to knock it off. It was like seeing a new side of things. These people were in leadership positions. I didn't know what to do, so I just got out of there.

Over the next few weeks, whenever my supervisor would come to my gate, I was nervous. Our previous interactions had been pleasant and respectful. But I had overheard a different side of it all. One of the other airmen was a K9 handler, and I already felt generally uneasy about him. I always felt this disdain from him, and he would make comments about me and one of the other Black airmen—how we were going around "thuggin'" or about the music we played.

I got quieter and quieter about the whole situation. Little things that my supervisor did prior to that day would have meant nothing to me, but now I distrusted it all. I was reading into a lot of things he said and did, wondering if there was something more beneath the surface. It was like the paranoia I had in high school, but it was also different. I felt like I had to keep an eye out over my shoulder for threats that were covert, if not overt.

I had come to Maxwell as a bright and lively airman. But after overhearing that conversation, I felt the paranoia and insomnia resurface. Up until joining the air force, I had outlived whatever came to get me. I had learned how to navigate all the feuding and fighting and crazy stuff around me. I knew how to avoid a fight and how to fight if I had to. I was good at protecting myself and knowing who I could trust. But I didn't know how to get through this. The military was different. It was full of people I didn't grow up with, all of whom had different motivations. There was no threat of harm or jail, but there were new, subtle undercurrents to worry about, like what I had overheard. It was a new world I didn't know how to navigate.

I felt trapped. I became depressed. I was in a distrustful mode of watching everybody. The bright-eyed enthusiasm of coming into the air force was gone. I no longer felt like I understood everything going on around me. I didn't have anyone to talk to about what I had overheard and how it made me feel. I had no one back home who I could really feel comfortable talking to, either.

These feelings of depression and frustration and paranoia continued. For a few weeks, my mind was running in so many different directions. I mostly worked the gates. Back in those days, we worked it alone, and it was busy, with thousands of cars coming through during our six- or eight-hour shifts. We really did not get much time to think, but whenever I was posted on the flight line, it gave me nothing but time to think. We were static, and radios or reading materials were not allowed.

One day I was on flight line patrol, which involved securing the aircraft on the base. It was the only patrol in which I could carry a rifle instead of the usual pistol. I decided I was going to take my life—right there in that patrol car. I remember looking at the rifle for hours, and my thoughts turned into actions as I started visualizing how I would do it. I remember rehearsing it and making sure I could reach the trigger. My thoughts seemed like they were walking off a cliff, and right before I stepped to the ledge, I caught myself.

But I couldn't do it.

What held me back, I think, was just the shock of looking at myself and realizing where I was at in my life. I couldn't believe what I was thinking. Never in my worst days had I wanted to do something like that. It snapped me out of it.

The next day they put me back on the same post, and I went through the same thing. Only this time the rehearsals continued, and now I had a little more courage. Instead of just practicing, I had a live round in the chamber with the weapon on fire. I got out of the car, walked around one of the aircrafts I was guarding, and made my decision: I was going to end this misery. I jumped back into the car, placed the barrel of the rifle in my mouth, and moved my finger over the trigger. I was going to take my life. But I wasn't able to do it.

On the third day, I wasn't working, so I called my mom. I told her she had to get me out of there, or I was going to kill myself. I guess it wasn't really fair to put her in that situation. She didn't travel. There was no way she could come get me.

My mom was hysterical. I was hysterical. I was practically tearing up in the phone booth. I couldn't get out of it, actually, as simple as it was to open. I started beating on the door to get out. The first sergeant, who was doing a dorm walk-through, found me in the phone booth. He didn't reprimand me. He just asked, "How can I help?" The first sergeant was an advisor on welfare for the airmen, and he had a diamond in his chevron to show it. I was a young airman in crisis, so he got me lined up with the care I needed.

That was the first time I formally dealt with a mental health issue. Where I came from, nobody talked about mental health. Looking back on what had happened with my mom after the preacher left her, I recognized that she went through a mental health crisis herself. But in the Black community in the eighties and nineties, *nobody* talked about mental health. Mental health was looked at as a bad thing or indicative of a weakness. Going to a therapist was foreign to me; I wouldn't even share those secrets with my mom. I never went to her and said something like, "Hey, I was in a bad drug deal last night, and someone had me at gunpoint. I could have died," or, "I have insomnia." In fact, I didn't even know I had insomnia. I just thought I couldn't sleep.

I'm happy that in my own family and circle of connections, I've seen people more open about mental health. But as a whole, even today, the Black community doesn't talk about it much. It's hard for some people to get their mind around accepting that mental health is real and that it's not a sign of weakness—it's something we need to address. Something I have dedicated my life to.

So I started going through a whole reckoning.

I felt comfortable talking to the first sergeant, but that wasn't enough. I was required to have a mental health appointment, but it just felt sterile and mechanical. I felt like I was in a doctor's office to get a checkup. Mental health was still taboo in the air force during the nineties. People were afraid of losing their security clearance or even their job. Not everyone in leadership was willing to help their subordinates get through their problems. There were comments like, "If they can't carry a gun, we don't want them around here." I am very thankful it's different today. There have been improvements in transparency and creating a safe space for vulnerability. But back then, I needed a better way to express myself and my pain.

I turned to the chaplain for guidance and support. I wasn't religious, but the chaplain provided a familiar setting—more so than a sterile room. My meetings with the chaplain were conversational. We talked about my childhood, the new world that I was in, and my feelings of being unable to navigate it. I confronted the fact that I had run away from home, where I was getting into trouble every day. I had barely made it out of Hardeeville. I realized there had been no mental break for me because I just jumped right into BMT and then the air force after that. I hadn't yet taken a moment to decompress or get my bearings.

There were parts that I still held back, though. I never really told anyone the complete story about what I had overheard. No one really knew what was going on. I wasn't brave enough to say there were racists in my squadron. If there was one thing the streets taught me, it was that retaliation was real. I think this is where the antisnitching culture originated. I almost thought I was losing my mind.

Truth be told, I arrived at Maxwell with a bit of an identity crisis. I had just come out of tech school, so full of life and enthusiasm—a world of difference from the hopelessness and apathy I had felt through high school and much of growing up.

My given name is Todd Maurice Simmons, but I always felt awkward with the name Todd. No Black man from the South was named Todd—or anyone of any skin color, for that matter. With an odd name like that, I was excited any time I heard about someone else with that name, like Todd Bridges on *Different Strokes* or the air force recruiter. Sometimes it's those little things that make a difference. It was our mutual name that helped the conversation get off the ground.

When I got into the military, I started using my middle name because I wanted to reinvent myself. It wasn't just about not liking Todd; it was about becoming a new person. This struggle plagued my every thought. I was only nineteen, but I felt like I was thirty. I did not identify with most of the airmen my age. I had seen so much and was in a different headspace.

One day I met a girl at the gate, and I told her my name was Maurice. She circled my gate twice and gave me her number. At this point in my life, I had some unhealthy relationships with women. I refused to have an actual girlfriend in high school because I was very distrustful of relationships, and the idea of commitment seemed foreign to me. I was in many relationships that ended when any sort of connection formed. But this girl and I had a fast-moving relationship. I was broke, but I would spend money on flowers or balloons for her. One time I went to the base exchange and bought her a ring, and she thought I had proposed to her. I just went with it. It was actually a friendship ring I bought for eighty-nine dollars, which was big money for an E2 in those days. I only bought it because she bought me a bracelet.

So there I was, somewhat engaged. One night we headed out to dinner. When we were at the table, I went over to the ATM to get money. I had taken my card and left my wallet open on the table. That's when she looked in my wallet at my driver's license. I came back, and she asked me, "Your name is Todd?"

At that moment, I was floored. It wasn't because I had been trying to lie to her, and she had found me out. It was that I had mentally checked out of being Todd. It was almost like she was asking me about a different person.

I didn't explain all that to her. I just told her it was my first name and that I was going by my middle name because I liked it better. Our relationship fell off when

I moved from Maxwell to my next assignment overseas, but I continued using Maurice for around three to four years. Even my wife was introduced to me as Maurice. My family got to know her over the phone, and they were confused when she would refer to me as Maurice. It kind of became a running joke.

The first sergeant talked to my commander about the opportunity for two airmen to go to Khobar Towers in Saudi Arabia. It would be a three-month assignment in Dhahran. I was asked if I wanted to go, and I said absolutely. After our conversations, I think he thought it would be good for me to get out of Alabama and see something different. Looking forward to that brought back some of that spark I had when I came into my first assignment, traveling from Fort Dix to Montgomery. Most airmen stayed at that base for two to four years, and that was a bleak prospect for me. How was I going to stick around these people? It was a relief and an opportunity to go somewhere else and get myself together.

6

A man who has no imagination has no wings.
—Muhammad Ali

In the fall of 1995, I was headed to Khobar Towers, Saudi Arabia, on a ninety-day deployment. I was feeling more excitement than I ever had in my life. I was headed to an exotic country like the far-off places I had seen in the encyclopedia. I had just survived a mental breakdown, and now I felt the same way I did the day I arrived at Maxwell. Adjustment in the military is real, and it takes time. My journey felt like it was starting on the right track.

The flight was long, and we stopped briefly in Egypt. The pilot told me to look out the window at the Great Pyramid of Giza. I couldn't believe I was nineteen years old and in Egypt, even though it was only for three hours.

Growing up, I saw movies about Cleopatra and documentaries about King Tut. It was like I was in another world. I remember the smell when they opened the doors to the plane and the immediate burst of hot air circulating. I took it all in and could not believe where I was.

I went to Saudi Arabia with the first sergeant, Sergeant Wells, who had helped me get back on my feet in Montgomery. He wasn't even assigned to security forces. He was a member of the maintenance unit, but he took a special interest in me and in helping me out. He would take me off the base into Dharan to eat at a Chinese restaurant. Like clockwork, he came and picked me up in his bright-red Ford pickup every week or so. This was the first time in my life I felt like I could trust someone when they said they were there for me. They were not mere words but action, which would quickly form my leadership style going forward. Words are great, but actions are critical.

There we were, in the Middle East, eating Chinese food. Those meetings became one of the major turning points in my life, if not the biggest, because Sergeant Wells was bringing empathy to the table.

Years later I would learn more about empathy. I even taught thousands on the power of empathy and connection through both virtual and in-person workshops. Though I didn't know it at the time, Sergeant Wells was using different parts of empathy to help me out. The cognitive component of empathy was all about sensing how someone else thinks about the world and finding common ground. The emotional component of empathy was resonating with what someone else was feeling. Empathetic concern was how someone expressed or offered help based on what the other person needed. Cognitive, emotional, and empathetic—he was doing all of that with me through our many conversations.

There was an older noncommissioned officer I lived with who was also Black. The apartments at Khobar Towers were set up with five bedrooms around a common area, so everyone living in our unit benefited from his guidance. This other NCO was an older staff sergeant who had been in the air force for a number of years already. He would sit on the couch and talk with us one-on-one, giving us tips about what we needed to do to progress in the air force. He was blunt with us, and the main thing that stood out about his advice was this: never let hard work go unnoticed. This was a formative time for me. I was being taught manhood. I was building healthy relationships with male figures and quickly rebuilding my trust in the air force. Years later, when I was in Alaska, I recalled his advice about proactivity. I was not step promoted because I was too quiet. I saw him again years later in Japan, when he was a master sergeant. We reconnected as we walked toward each other down a hallway. By that point, I was just one rank behind him, and I even eventually caught up with him. When we met, he said he was proud of me. That accolade was very telling about his character and the genuine care he had for us.

Sergeant Wells and this older NCO never knew how much they influenced me. For most of my life, I had just kind of made it by going through the motions. Even during BMT, although I developed a better sense of self-worth, I still hadn't hit some kind of turning point about what I wanted to do with my life in the long term. At Maxwell I had stumbled into depression after overhearing the racist comments, and I slipped back into paranoia. I didn't tell Sergeant Wells about the rifle and how close I came to committing suicide, but he sensed it in me. He knew something was wrong, and he knew how to fix it.

We went to this Chinese restaurant about a half dozen times. Each time I was unknowingly opening up more and more. The conversations were never sterile. It did not feel like we were in the military. We talked about life, sports, the heat, and I was interested in his twenty-year career that had taken him all over the globe. One particular dinner we had before returning to Maxwell was the scene of a pivotal, life-changing conversation for me. Sergeant Wells asked me what I wanted to do—meaning, what did I want to do with my life. I wasn't sure. I had met new friends. Maybe I wanted to go to school. Maybe not. I was terrified of any kind of academic situation, like getting recertified as a security police member, which was a yearly requirement. The recertification test for security forces consisted of a written test, a verbal test, and a practical exam. The practical part was easy for me, but the oral piece was always challenging, especially the requisite memorization to recite answers verbatim.

Sergeant Wells had never brought that question up before getting to know me. He had worked at sensing me out and learning how to resonate with my feelings. He knew how to ask the most important question anyone had ever asked me: What did I want to do with my life?

And what made that question so meaningful was not the question itself but the authority he had to ask it. He had gotten to know me and my story. That connection gave him authority to ask that question, and it created the space for me to believe whatever response he would give my answer.

I said I just wanted to serve in the air force. I didn't have anywhere else to go, and I didn't have any money. I wanted to get away from Montgomery. And then I added that I wanted to see the world. I had changed my mind about needing to stay close to home.

When I said that, I was thinking about how incredible it had been to get out and see the world. Every Saturday in Dharan we went through the local shops buying trinkets, and it fascinated me to walk through the food and spices of the bazaar and to taste the kebabs and the shawarma. I fell in love with Middle Eastern food and the idea of seeing the world.

Sometimes we would work the gates with Saudi guards: one American and three Saudis. One night they brought this huge silver pan with them. It had a layer of rice, a layer of vegetables, and a layer of baked chicken—it smelled incredible. I was sitting there eating my American cheese sandwich. They were sitting on the floor and kept asking me if I wanted to join them. I said no again and again for about thirty minutes, and then I finally said yes. I looked around for a fork and knife, but they were eating by scooping it all up with bread. There was a fellowship about the experience. They made tea, and we had that together. These were the kinds of experiences I would never get living in Hardeeville.

Sergeant Wells pulled out a napkin from the dispenser. I had been to Egypt already. I was living in Dhahran, Saudi Arabia. What could be bigger? He wrote down eight bases and then went into them in detail: three in Japan, and one each in Alaska, Germany, England, Korea, and Iceland. It took me back to being seven years old, reading those encyclopedias in my mom's house. I never would've had that much curiosity about the world if I hadn't immersed myself in the encyclopedias or watched National Geographic on TV. I loved watching documentaries about African tribes and different parts of the world. Indiana Jones was one of my heroes, but I never thought I would get an opportunity to go to these places. Him writing down those bases all over the world and hearing about each one was like flipping through those pages. I remember asking, "Man, I can do all that?"

Yes. Yes, I could.

For every one of those bases he put down on the napkin, he told me a story about his time there and what the culture was like in that country. He had been in the air force for twenty-four years, so he had a lot of life experience. But he also told me that it would be good for me to get overseas, not just in terms of experiencing new places but for my own well-being. The people on overseas bases are more tight knit, and the camaraderie was better because they were all Americans together in a foreign place.

He wrote down Korea as a place to go, but in parentheses he indicated I should only go when I was mature. Korea was notorious in the nineties as a party place. At the time, I didn't really pay attention to that part. I kind of wrote it off. But he had the believability to answer the question for me, so I took his advice and didn't go until I was thirty-four.

I took that napkin back with me to Alabama, and I would say I lived my life by that napkin for the rest of the time I was in the air force. In fact, I pretty much followed that napkin for seventeen consecutive years. The principle of that napkin was this: get out and see the world. Building a relationship based on trust can be a game changer. Positions and titles mean absolutely nothing unless there is credibility and an open exchange of ideas. I actually laminated that napkin and pinned it to my desk while I worked in Alaska and later when I worked in Japan. At some point, when we moved to Japan, I lost track of it. I might have it boxed up somewhere.

I followed everything he wrote on that napkin. I went to England, Japan, the Middle East, and I waited to go to Korea until I was more mature. I did everything on that napkin because I believed what Sergeant Wells said. He knew what I needed and when I needed it. He didn't just walk up out of nowhere and order me to do something or suggest it would be good for me without knowing me.

When we got back to Montgomery, I almost had a little bit of a setback. I quickly reverted to feeling like I was in survival mode. My friends were different; my environment was different. Old feelings started to return. Sergeant Wells followed up and asked me if I had filled out the dream sheet with the command support staff. I had asked the sergeant in command support, but he said something like, "You just got here. You ain't going anywhere." I was deflated. But Sergeant Wells marched me back there and pretty much ordered him to help me fill it out. I filled it out along the lines of what was written on the napkin.

Nearly 40 days later, I got orders to RAF Lakenheath in England. So just 367 days from when I drove through the gates of Air University, where I came within a few pounds of pressure on a trigger from taking my own life, and then after going to Saudi Arabia, where I got in touch with what I wanted to do with my life, I was headed overseas to live in the United Kingdom.

Receiving the Southwest Asia Campaign Medal.

7

It's hard to beat a person who never gives up.
—Babe Ruth

SO, WHEN AN OPPORTUNITY CAME, I took it. I had made the decision to leave Montgomery and go overseas. I arrived at RAF Lakenheath in February 1996. What a culture shock that was. Even though I had lived in Saudi Arabia, I had mostly stayed on the base.

I made a friend on the flight to England, Mario White, who became one of my best friends. We were always pushing each other toward success and education. We made rank together, and we were promoted to non-commissioned officers together at the beginning of 1999. This was the first true friendship I had in the military, and it's been my longest friendship. He was the best man at my wedding.

It was amazing to be in England, a country with so much history. I loved its history, and I fell in love with the place. For me, the biggest realizations I had there were about myself, about race, and about how I fit into the bigger picture of a society outside the small southern town where I grew up. Incidentally, I was still using Maurice as my first name. This was part of me trying to create a different persona.

There was a military club on an adjacent base, RAF Mildenhall, which was called the Galaxy Club. It was world famous in the eighties and nineties, and not just in the military. Even though it was on a base, parts of the base were open to the public, including the club, and tons of British girls would come through there on the weekend. Prior to leaving Maxwell, I remember speaking to the person who had helped me transition to England saying, "You are young, Black, and single. Get ready to have a great time here." I had no idea what he meant.

I had only been in the country for about four days, and someone suggested we go to the club. I'll never forget it. There were hundreds of people in that club, White and Black, listening to hip-hop and R&B. It was easy to spot the long line of British girls waiting to get signed in. If you were not a club member, a club member had to sign you into the club. This created a long line of girls waiting for guys to pass and sign them into the club. It was something I had never seen before, and it was completely intimidating at first. Where I grew up, the idea of having a relationship, a close friendship, or even talking to a White female was not commonplace. So this was a culture shock. But here everyone was mixing and mingling. I saw Black and White people, GIs and airmen, Brits and Americans. I remember the first drink I bought for a girl there was a White Russian. I saw the bartender pouring it, but I didn't really know what was in it.

It was in England that I started meeting Black guys who had White girlfriends. I had seen interracial couples in Hardeeville, but very infrequently. I started dating a British girl who I had seen at the club and who came around the barracks. What caught my attention about her was a total lack of reservation about dating someone of a different race. There was no embarrassment or shame about being together if we were out. I remember someone calling me a "bloke" one time when I was with her and thinking that maybe it was a derogatory term for a Black man. I was from a small southern town where publicly dating a White girl was still taboo, so I just figured that's what it was about, though it turned out "bloke" was just a term for a young man.

This girl invited me to her house to meet her family. Back in Hardeeville, I rarely went to a White person's house. I had known guys who sneaked around with White girls, but never in front of anyone else. And here I was, this twenty-year-old Black kid dating a White girl and getting invited over to her house. Dinner was initially weird to me. I was the only person of color at the table. Her family's kindness shocked me. I remember thinking, *This is strange.*

While I was in England, I bought a car to get around—a Ford Fiesta that cost me $250. The engine would shut off if I stopped too long at a light, so I had to coast up to intersections and hope for the light to turn green real quick. One day I drove over to her house, and her mom and dad seemed to be leaving for the weekend, saying that maybe they'd be back on Sunday—and that I was welcome to stay over. I was like, *Huh? Did they really just say that?* It blew my mind.

Our relationship only lasted about three months. A big part of the reason it didn't work out was because of my own discomfort with an interracial relationship at the time. I could go anywhere in the world as a member of the air force, but I still lacked self-confidence. Before that whole experience, I was not willing to get involved in an interracial relationship on a personal level, so this was a huge step forward for me in terms of broadening my worldview.

This squadron was different from the one in Maxwell, which had been mostly Caucasian and smaller. There were about 120 airmen in the squadron at Maxwell, and here there were 500 people of all different races. I saw African Americans in leadership positions. I saw people like me all around, from E3 young airmen to officers all the way up the leadership chain. I felt like possibilities were opening up for me, and I loved the work I was doing on the base. There was a Black captain and a Black flight chief directly in my chain of command. Until then, I hadn't seen so many Blacks in leadership roles, so this gave me a new sense of hope.

And then there was also the cultural diversity. I was from a small town in South Carolina. I had friends like Mario, who was from Maryland. I had friends from Atlanta, DC, and Compton, California. Before that, the only thing I knew about Compton was what I saw on TV. Diversity and inclusion are powerful things.

I did not get along with my first roommate. He was a throwback to what I knew from being raised in the South. As much as I was excited about what I saw on the surface in England, there was always a door number two waiting around the corner to show us the realities of the world. He was an aircraft mechanic, so I'm not sure why he was even in the dorms for security forces. He let the room get pretty filthy, and it really upset me. One evening I brought the British girl I was dating to our room, and he made a comment that she might date me, but she would never let her parents know about me. Of course, he was wrong about that. At this point, I would say I was growing up. I had an extreme temper when I joined the air force and never hesitated to step up to a fight, but I was changing. I remember going to the dorm manager and basically saying to him, "Sir, I see two choices: either you move me, or you move him. The third option is going to be violence, so I am coming to you to let you know what's going on." He laughed and said he would move him out that week. My second roommate was from Brooklyn, and we got along much better. Even though we were both Black, we had grown up worlds apart. He introduced me to new music. I knew the culture of the South, which he had never experienced. This is why I love studying and talking about diversity and inclusion. We tend to think about it as simply Black and White. I learned just as much from Paige being from New York as I learned from immersing myself in British culture through my girlfriend at the time. Paige was older and a student of the arts and Black culture. He introduced me to art and even gave me my first piece of art, which I still have over twenty-three years later.

I got to talking with people during duty. Being with another person for ten to twelve hours made communication essential. I was sharing hip-hop with White airmen from Kentucky and listening to bluegrass for the first time. It was a cultural exchange.

One night I was on patrol in a truck with a guy reading a book. To make some conversation, I asked him what he was reading. He showed me this book by Donald Goines, *Never Die Alone*. At that point in my life, I had *never* read a book cover to cover. He told me a little bit about the book and about Goines, a Black author writing about some hellacious things. I was intrigued. He gave me the book, and the story resonated with me. Though it was fictional, the setting and the characters were familiar. I read the whole book in five days. In fact, I liked it so much I went over to the convenience store and bought more books. My reading started from that genre and then took off into biographies about Black leaders, which transitioned into books about leadership and self-improvement.

I was trying to educate myself on things I didn't get growing up. The only thing I had read before that was military regulations. Did it take me longer to finish that first book? Yes. Did I have to go back to understand certain parts? Yes. But I finished it, and that launched my interest in reading—something I had never really done in school.

It was at RAF Lakenheath that I met Master Sergeant Dixon, who had a BA in English, and he really helped transform my ability to communicate effectively—another thing that school had not really provided me. I was a desk sergeant with three levels of certification, essentially an emergency dispatcher. A lot of administrative multitasking was required of me, with phones going off, alarms ringing, and endless reports to fill out. My elevation to this position was a little bit controversial, and there were older folks who had said no to the idea, but Sergeant Dixon gave me a chance. Later, as a leader in the air force and as a business owner, I would follow this motto of giving people a chance based on their hunger. My motto became: "I can teach anyone skills, but I can't teach drive and motivation." I would seek out those who were hungry and wanted to open the door to opportunity. That was me in this opportunity. Master Sergeant Dixon provided the crack, and I kicked the door wide open.

One White staff sergeant in particular did not want me there, and his treatment of me sure showed it. He'd give me snappy orders for mundane tasks, like, "Take out the trash," or, "Make coffee." I always made the worst coffee to spite him. He wasn't really trying to train me. I think he was just trying to bring on my attitude and kick me out. Back then people used words they don't use in the military anymore, like *dumbass* or *stupid*. But I never let him see me sweat. I never let him get to me.

Despite him trying to push my buttons, I kept training. I kept watching him and learning. I would even come in on my days off to learn as much as I could. This really pissed him off. He thought he controlled my ability to learn. For me, it wasn't about the position; it was about not letting someone else dictate the level of success I could achieve. This was another real turning point in my life, when I once again asked, *Why not me?* Growing up, I had asked why I wasn't somebody born into wealth or privilege. After high school I asked why I had just narrowly avoided getting trapped in the drug game. And now I was asking that question from a place with a little more opportunity on the horizon. I saw people excelling around me. That question wasn't coming from a negative place. Rather, it came from place that could spur me on to achieve something greater. *Why not me?*

We had to type up a nightly blotter of forms and reports. At this point, I was still limited in terms of formal education, and here I was, faced with this huge administrative task. At first I struggled with it. I had templates I would use, like samples from other airmen. I'd go around and ask, "Can you give me copies of your reports?" It took me a while to learn the ropes. Sergeant Dixon was patient. He knew that the staff sergeant I was training under was hazing me and wanted me to fail. But I didn't ask for help. Sergeant Dixon would come in and mark my reports up with red pens, and then I'd have to stay up long after work and fix things.

This went on for several months. He would mark it down to a point where I was like, *Wow.* It was really confronting me with my own educational deficiencies in terms of expressing myself. Over time, there was less red ink. But my goal was to get a *perfect* blotter. It took about a year. I didn't understand when I signed up for that role that I would practically be going through an English class. He'd zero in on little details, like don't use the word *that*—use something more specific. He'd take apart the grammar. I learned so much in that year, and it really propelled my career. Advancement in the air force was largely about articulation with written words. Sergeant Dixon really changed my life and my career with the way he coached me through my writing.

During my first two years in England, I went all over the place. I went to Morón, Spain, near Seville, for three months for temporary duty. There was definitely some culture shock there. I remember one day we decided to check out some of the beaches that weren't too far away. As a twenty-one-year-old American, I could not believe that Europeans went to the beach without clothes. It was in Spain, actually, that I had a run-in with my bunkmate from BMT.

We were both on our second assignment in England, and we were both sent to Spain to do security on an American base. I was out on the town with a few other airmen, and we had been having some drinks in a bar in Seville. I didn't even realize he was also in the bar. A lot of the bars in Spain were below street level. As we walked up the stairs back to the street, he bumped into me and mumbled a comment that sounded like it had some racial undertones. We got into each other's faces. He grabbed me and tried to throw me down the stairs, so I grabbed him, pinned him down, and started choking him before we got pulled apart by the other people with us. I could see the fear in his eyes. We were not in BMT anymore—what were the odds? This was the second time I could *absolutely* feel animosity coming at me because of race, and it was the same individual exuding it. But this time around, I got my say in the matter. For the rest of our time together in Spain and England, he avoided me and eventually left the air force a few years later. He was a wake-up call to me early in my career. I was a little naive when I joined the air force. I believed every man and woman in uniform was the same, but this situation proved me wrong. We may all give our lives for this country, but not everyone sees you as an equal.

I really wanted to see as much of every place as I could. Most of my friends liked going to clubs locally, but I wanted to travel. One time we got a group together and went to Scotland. I'll never forget Hogmanay, which is how they celebrate New Year's in Scotland. It's a celebration that is one of the biggest in the world. We took a bus up north, and our trip included a stay at the Royal Scott Hotel. I went with an interracial couple I knew from tech training and another airman friend.

The Scottish folks were lively. Though it was cold outside, the whole town was one big friendly party. One of my favorite movies was *Braveheart*, so this was a real cool visual experience to be celebrating in the shadow of Edinburgh Castle. We were out there having a great time with hundreds of thousands of other people that night. We were hopping around to different bars, clubs, and pubs. Drinking is legal at age eighteen, and I had only gotten really drunk a few times since joining the military. Drinking was not new to me, as I started drinking around the age of fifteen. But there were people buying us drinks, and after a while we got separated. It was cold, snowing, and I had no money whatsoever. I remember trying to get cash out of the ATM and not having enough money in my checking account for ten pounds.

There I was in downtown Edinburgh. I had no idea where my friends were. I was drunk and lost. I think my survival skills kicked in. I was walking around, trying to find an ATM that would let me take out what little cash I had, when I ended up in this neighborhood far outside the city. I was cold. My shoes were wet from the snow. I was starting to get scared—I didn't know if the cold was sobering me up or if I was experiencing hypothermia. But there I was, just walking down the sidewalk, not knowing what I was going to do. As a Black kid, there was no way I was going to knock on someone's door at three in the morning.

Suddenly, there was this guy walking toward me. I think he had a ponytail. I remember thinking, *Is this a modern-day Jack the Ripper approaching me?* It was dark, and he was wearing a hoodie. I could barely see his face. My street smarts kicked in. I asked myself, *Am I going to have to fight this dude in this cold-ass street?* My goal was just to walk past him, but he stopped me and asked if I was okay. Clearly, I was lost. I said I was just trying to find my hotel. He said there were no hotels around there. As I was thinking about walking back to the city, he asked me where I was staying, and I said the Royal Scott Hotel. He flagged down a taxi and told the driver where I needed to go. He paid for the fare. This was another lesson on the power of empathy. He practiced extreme empathetic concern by knowing what I needed at the time I needed it. He had the believability through his actions by flagging down a cab and paying for it and walking away with no questions asked. This was another major reflection point on my journey.

I walked into the hotel lobby and made my way back to the room, and there was my friend, snoring in his bed like nothing was wrong! Meanwhile, I was walking all over the city through the snow and cold trying to get back. But anyway, when we woke up, we had an eight-hour ride on the bus back to base—and that's when I knew how much I had drank the night before. I'll never forget it: We took over the back of the bus, and I was curled up on the seat, just thinking, *Let this be over.* I knew I was out of money. When we stopped at a gas station, four hours into the ride, I did not get off the bus. I couldn't. But this British girl sitting in the rear of the bus with us brought me a sandwich, juice, and water. It was a nice gesture, and I ended up taking her out on a date, though that relationship didn't go anywhere.

One day this friend of mine, Colby, called me up while I was on patrol to respond to a nonemergency incident. I walked into his room to find nothing much amiss and said, "Hey, what's going on?" He was there with a girlfriend who would later become his wife and another girl he wanted me to meet. I said, "What?" That was quite a way to get me over to his room to meet her—it caught me off guard.

Colby's girlfriend was always telling me about her large group of Black female friends. She was always trying to hook me up, and I would never take her up on it. I think she knew I would brush her suggestions off if she tried to set me up with someone, so they pulled a fast one on me.

This girl was kind of quiet. I was on duty at the time, so I couldn't really sit there and chat. I was standing, armed, with all my law enforcement gear on. I said, "Okay, I met her. Well, I'm going back to work."

But then she started walking outside with me. We were talking. There were no cell phones back in that day, so I told her that if we walked down to my room, just down the hall, I could get a pen and paper, and we could trade numbers. I remember her number was really long—that's just the way it was in England.

I took her number and told her I would call her the next day. But the next day, I ended up having to do some training at that time. I called her and left a message on her answering machine to let her know that I couldn't call her at our prearranged time. For some reason, that courtesy was the key to the kingdom. She thought it was very nice.

On our first date, we went to a Mexican restaurant at a British pub. We started talking and had a great conversation; I really liked her personality. In some ways, we could understand each other's past lives. There were similarities in the way we grew up, even though we grew up in different parts of the country. She was twenty-one years old and already had a daughter who was out in New Mexico with her mom. She had been in a bad relationship with someone who was kicked out of the military—incidentally, someone I knew.

Initially, I was not sure about the idea of dating her. She had a kid, but that wasn't a huge concern for me. If anything, it was more of a concern for her because she would be letting someone come into her daughter's life if it became a serious relationship. I think it was more about relationships being difficult for me, probably because of how I was raised. I never had anyone drawing me in close growing up, so I would always be standoffish in relationships. But we hit it off. We ate Mexican food, walked around the park, and talked. We ended up spending quite a bit of time together.

I don't think we skipped a day of seeing each other after that first date. She did try to break up with me a few times. Maybe things seemed to be moving too fast for both of us. Our friends were kind of pushy about getting their friends into relationships because they really liked having a whole group in which couples could all get together socially. She had just gotten out of a bad relationship and had a one-year-old daughter. And as for me, I wasn't so used to the idea of opening up in a serious relationship. But we always got back together.

Master Sergeant Dixon, who I had definitely hit it off with, was taking a team to Bosnia and Herzegovina, which was then embroiled in the Balkan Wars. He asked me if I wanted to deploy. This was obviously not a great time to be in a new relationship and volunteer to deploy. But I really enjoyed deploying. It gave me a sense a purpose and made me feel more connected to the military. I said yes, and we went down there about a month later. He gave me the job of a desk sergeant for the flight line—the runways where the planes and helicopters landed and took off. We were set up in an old Russian military building. Meanwhile, my future wife, whom I had only been dating for a few short months, had been deployed to Italy. We had been inseparable since our first date at the Mexican restaurant, and now we were both deployed in two distinct areas supporting the same mission.

Bosnia deployment, 1998

I was a newly promoted senior airman, E4. We were running these humanitarian convoys to NATO orphanages and living out of a tent ourselves. A lot of the children in these orphanages had parents killed during the ethnic cleansing. I was twenty-one years old and immersed in something of this magnitude, though at the time, I don't really think I internalized it. I felt alive. We were helping people and having a positive effect. Fast-forward to February 2020 at a chief induction ceremony at Hickam Air Force Base: I was talking to a young female staff sergeant who grew up in Kosovo during that time, and she told me that during the war, when she was just four years old, she and her family walked to a refugee camp and lived there until they emigrated to the United States. Her telling me that story and understanding what kind of part I had in helping that situation made our work come full circle. This is another example of being willing to listen to the quietest voices in the room—the willingness to have an empathic ear. In 2014

I developed and perfected a method I call "pulling the string." I find people who seem to have trouble connecting with others. I have a theory that most people will only tell you two to five things about themselves in a normal face-to-face introduction. How do you pull the strings from there? I sometimes say more about myself in order to ease the situation and hope the other person will share more. It is all about finding an intersecting connection that will start a connection point that can build a relationship. That's what happened during my conversation with the staff sergeant at Hickam. It started with where she was from and what she did for a living. I proceeded to tell her all about where I grew up, and the connection of her coming to the United States from Kosovo was the thread we needed to expose to start a real connection. That brief seventeen-minute interaction led to an emotional connection that gave both of us a sense of purpose and reflection that continues today.

Bosnia NATO recognition

My future wife and I talked on the phone when we could. Before the advent of cell phones, we had morale calls. We got fifteen minutes, three times a week. That's obviously changed with cell phones and FaceTime. Our conversations were short. Email was new, so we didn't really use it to communicate. There were no apps and no texting. Our times had to line up the right way. Some operators were cool, while others were hard to work with and would surprise us with a sixty-second warning right before our time was up, whether or not we were in the middle of working out something important.

The distance was difficult. We started wondering if we had to break up. I was feeling depressed and unsure if it would work out. Sergeant Dixon found out about all this after I got into a big fight with a tentmate over refilling a heater. Tensions were high, it was cold, and it was easy to get set off. In those days, you could have a fistfight in the tent, bloody each other up, and go about your business and shake hands the next day. I had my fair share of those altercations.

So, when he found out what else was bothering me, he asked where she was based. I told him she had returned to England. He said there was a C130 transport headed to Germany at least every other day and that he could set me up to get cross training there as a paralegal. That was something I had wanted, and I was still within my window to get it. Although I liked being a cop for the first three years, I had really become interested in the law and daydreamed about becoming a lawyer. He would also talk to her leadership and see if they would let her meet me there. In the meantime, he told me to call her and see if she was interested. She said yes, and Sergeant Dixon set it all up.

We met in Germany for a visit. It had been 120 days of knowing each other, only 60 of which involved seeing each other in person. We got engaged and then married back in England at Bury Saint Edmunds just four and half months after meeting one another. My friends Mario and Demond Harper were my best men.

Wedding Day

I wasn't committed to the air force as a lifer. Sometimes in the air force we ask each other, "When did you *commit* to the air force?" which essentially means, "When did you decide to make this your career?" I wasn't a career airman at that point. As far as education went, I took one college class while I was on duty. It was a distance learning course, with fourteen VHS tapes, followed by a test. I failed the class horribly. I had to pay hundreds of dollars back to the government, and that messed me up. It was kind of a setback in terms of my attempt to get a more formalized education. It made me feel like I wasn't who I thought I was.

I wanted to stay overseas. I was still looking at this napkin from my time in Saudi Arabia. Where to next? But the stakes were different now. I was married, and I was walking into a family. It was no longer just about me, and that was a foreign feeling. I had always focused on protecting and taking care of myself. I was doing well in the squadron. I was on cloud nine, really. I found out I had made staff sergeant. It was 1998, and it was still difficult to get promoted quickly in the air force. In fact, of the thirteen who got promoted to staff sergeant, I was only one of two who made it the first time around, scoring a ninety-two on the test. I had used the same learning methods I had learned I could leverage in BMT, studying the same information for hours at a time. I was not naive about my learning challenges, and I believe that is what gave me the advantage over others. I knew I was probably on the lower end of the rosters when it came to academics, but I considered myself to be at the very top when it came to work ethic and persistence. I did not have to be the smartest in the room, but I had to be the hardest working in order to survive. I think those lessons came from my family, who worked multiple jobs to get ahead.

And my personal life was going well, too. I was newly married, with a one-and-half-year-old stepdaughter. I was proud to be any kind of father figure. We were planning to go to Germany, but then my wife got an assignment to Alaska. As it turned out, Alaska was on the napkin, but Germany was on that napkin higher up. My wife was smart. At that point in her career, there was no stopping her. When we moved in with each other, we bought an entertainment center to put our stuff on. When we unpacked our things, there she was, taking trophy after trophy out of the box. It seemed like she won everything, and she had served less time in the air force. I took out one certificate printed on purple paper, which I had kept in a folder: airman of the month. That was all I had.

I credit my wife for motivating me to do better. She was an airman on fire. So I decided it made sense to go with her idea. She knew what she was doing. She headed off to Eielson Air Force Base just outside of Fairbanks, and I stayed in England five extra months because my time wasn't up.

8

You must do the things you think you cannot do.
—Eleanor Roosevelt

When my wife and stepdaughter moved to Alaska in August, I moved into somewhat of a dream home: a small flat over a fish and chips shop in Brandon. It was the kind of picturesque apartment one could picture in a small English village or over High Street in London, with its pubs and small grocery stores sprinkled with kabob shops. I think this was the first time I felt like a productive adult. I had overcome so many challenges, and here I was four short years later. I bought my first brand-new car and was living the life I imagined when I joined the air force. Was this finally it? I put in leave to visit them in Alaska for Christmas. In December I landed in Fairbanks, and all I saw around me was a complete whiteout. Everything was covered in snow. I had never seen anything like it.

My wife had driven thirty-six miles to pick me up. As we drove back to the base, we passed along a desolate road. Halfway through, there was a town that was actually called North Pole, Alaska. Its main street had a Blockbuster and grocery store. Eielson Air Force Base was in the middle of nowhere. I remember thinking to myself, *This is going to be the next three years of my life.* It was at least fifty to sixty degrees *below* zero. During those two weeks of leave for Christmas and New Year's, I felt deflated. Why did we come here instead of going to Germany?

In the summer, I saw a different side of Alaska. It was a beautiful place, and I think this started a love of the outdoors for my wife and me. Every assignment since then we've made sure we could enjoy hiking and being outdoors. I started playing golf there, of all places. We took a train to Denali. I even learned to appreciate the winter. I had fished in the South and already liked fishing, so I learned how to fish on the dozens of lakes on base.

After that two-week leave, I went back to England and made arrangements to wrap up our stay there. I shipped my car to Alaska. It was my first ever brand-new car, with plastic on the seats. It was a 1999 Honda Civic I had bought through the military exchange. I arrived in Alaska as a newly promoted staff sergeant. I remember looking around at the squadron that was there and thinking what a change it was. I had just left a five-hundred-airmen squadron in the United Kingdom that was very diverse, and now I was moving to a state in which diversity was almost nonexistent. No one in a leadership position was minority or female across the base.

I felt like I needed to readjust my mind from where I had been for the three previous years. At Lakenheath I had developed a diverse friend group. In Alaska I didn't fit in with the conversations around me—about moose hunting, for example. This was a small squadron with people who had been there for a while. I felt like I needed to get my bearings again. There was one other Black staff sergeant, an E5 NCO who was a little older than me. He had been in Alaska for a while and knew the lay of the land.

I was a desk sergeant, but now I had people I supervised. I had to take responsibility for them, and I was proud to take on this challenge. At the same time, the idea of continuing my formal education continued to linger in my mind. The only college classes I had taken were the VHS course I had failed in England and one in-person criminal justice class that I enjoyed. Even though I didn't get college credits out of it, I did have a lot of education around communication because Sergeant Dixon had taught me so much about writing, and I had been reading books. That progress made me think that maybe I was ready to start pursuing formal education again. My wife was a great airman and full of aspirations, but I was still not considering becoming a lifer in the air force. We looked at our goals together. At this time my wife was a senior airman E4 and wanted to become an officer. But before that, she wanted to finish her degree and was taking three classes per semester. About six months after arriving in Alaska, I started taking classes again, too, after mapping out how I could get a college degree. There were a lot of people getting degrees at Eielson Air Force Base since there was nothing much else to do there if you did not hunt or fish, especially in the dead of winter. The sign-up sheet for classes was literally a waiting list. For many airmen, school also served as a social outlet. A four-hour class at nearby Wayland Baptist University might be the only time anyone saw twenty to thirty other people.

I remember my degree plan showing me the credits and classes I needed to get a BS, and it looked daunting. It was well over 120 credits. I took the easy classes first, mostly to get used to the rhythm of school again. I tried to get college algebra out of the way, and then I dropped it. I took it again six months later and failed it. I was devastated. I was taking it at a nearby army base, and I remember the instructor constantly telling me I wasn't going to get it. He wasn't trying to be discouraging; my math skills were at a deficit because of the way I had neglected them in high school. In order to pass college algebra, I needed to go back and learn some foundational math. Without doing that, there was no way I could learn the concepts needed to pass college algebra. This knocked me off my high. I was actually depressed over the fact that I had so much to overcome. How could I have gone so many years through an education system and learned basically nothing? It made me think about those conversations with my friends who had dropped out of high school to start working in the service industry or sell drugs. Were they right? Was school a waste of time?

Absolutely not! Even though I barely got into the air force and faced huge barriers learning things that came simple to others, I would not have had the opportunity to join if I did not have a diploma. That diploma represented a foundational opportunity. Dropping out limits options in an already limited-option environment, so no, they were not right.

That all seemed pretty daunting, and it made me feel depressed. So I parked algebra in the corner. In the meantime, I pursued the other courses for my degree in human services and criminal justice. I loved sociology and social work. But because Wayland Baptist University was a private university, I also had to take classes on New Testament and Old Testament studies. I had grown up with my family being involved in the local church. But Bible studies presented a different challenge. I passed the New Testament class with a C and the Old Testament with a B. I think the only reason I passed the Old Testament course was because it was a lunchtime class taught by a professor who was more of a storyteller than an academic. But the New Testament class was taught by a theologian with a PhD. The exams were ten pages of filling in the blank for different verses, so we had to know them verbatim. I would barely get through some of these tests, even with a lot of studying. After the experience with the pastor who married my mom and then left her, I was not deeply religious. I didn't even attend church in high school. I had gotten back into church in England, but I had some experiences there that also left me distrustful. Generally speaking, I did not read the Bible much until these classes.

Our first year on the base went by quickly. My wife and I were taking classes. During our second year on the base, we went to South Carolina on vacation, and it was the first time my family met my wife. My wife was from New Mexico and had never really experienced the beach. So my daughter stayed with my mom, and I took my wife to the beach in Jacksonville. My family was a little closed-minded when it came to interracial relationships, and I think that idea prompted the reservations I had with dating British girls when I first landed in England. When we arrived in South Carolina, a family member told me they had bets that my wife was White, not Black. I was confused because they spoke to my wife on the phone several times, but she did sound unlike anyone from the South, because she was not from the South.

I found out my wife was pregnant in a roundabout way when we were back in Alaska. One day she had to go to Fairbanks to get some dry cleaning, which was around thirty miles away from the base. I remember it was snowing, and I said I didn't think she should go. Well, she ended up going, and a little while later I got a call from an EMT. Her car had flipped over five times, with our daughter in the back seat. Thankfully, both of them were uninjured, except for a gash on my wife's forehead. They released her from the ambulance, and I took her to the base hospital to check her out, where we found out she was pregnant.

She doubled down on her education to get it finished before she gave birth. She started taking four or five classes per semester. I had always been in awe of her; when she gave birth to our daughter, she turned in homework the next day because she had a deadline to meet for officer training school.

We made a decision that I was going to be a civilian, and she would be an officer in the air force. I was actually scheduled to go up for a promotion to E6, but I didn't even take the study material out of the packet. I didn't get the promotion because I didn't bother studying. But I was still going hard with the classes because I wanted to get my degree. There were times I had to go back and learn the foundation of something in order to catch up to where I needed to be at the college level. I was good with English. I was not strong in math or chemistry or statistics. If the requirement for a course was one semester, it became three semesters for me. I would have to take the high school course, then the entry-level college course, and then the course I needed to graduate. This resulted taking three classes to pass one course. I wasn't able to show up to just any class and plug into the basics because of my educational deficit.

While we were in Alaska, I took my first of several second jobs to offset the cost of the college classes we were taking. The military only funded 75 percent, and my wife and I were taking up to six classes together, plus the costs of books, so it was a huge financial commitment. I remember working at the local base club at night and on the weekends. One particular night, I remember working at the front, checking the identification of entering customers. I remember a group I knew from around the base of young Black males my age come in. We all spoke and exchanged greetings. After they were through, I heard them laughing and saying, "He must be broke working here. There is no way I would embarrass myself working here, where people could see me." For a brief moment, I got into my feelings, and then I laughed it off. When I was sixteen years old, I had thousands of dollars in my pocket, owned several cars before I was eighteen, and wore the latest fashions and jewelry. I was severely unhappy with my life. I was proud to be earning six dollars an hour to support my family and my future. This was definitely not a negative version of *Why not me.* Rather, the question was, "Why not you?"

Nobody knew I wasn't committed to the air force as a lifer. I was one of the top performing NCOs in the squadron, and I was even NCO of the year two years running. I was stratified on my EPRs as the number one staff sergeant in the squadron. I even took the test to go to Officer Training School (OTS), which was a humbling experience. People around me were pushing me to do more in the air force, but I had other passions I wanted to pursue. I would never turn down an opportunity or let anyone know my intentions were to separate. I did not want to burn any bridges. I had every recommendation, award, and requirement met to become an officer in the air force, but I could not score high enough on the math portion of the test. It was interesting how this experience would come up seventeen years later, when I was at the helm of education in the air force. But I decided I wouldn't chase promotion at that time by trying to move up the ranks. Instead, I would try to get my degree.

I was going strong with my classes when my wife gave birth to our daughter, Amari. We had to go to the army hospital in Fairbanks, and we were there for a few days because she was going off and on into labor. On our last day there, we walked around for a few hours until she walked herself into labor because we didn't want to keep driving back and forth thirty-six miles.

Bringing my daughter Amari home from the hospital

After that, my wife hit her last class, which just so happened to be college algebra. She asked if I wanted to take it with her, but I wasn't ready to take it. She decided to take it online because she had just given birth. This was still 2001, so I couldn't believe anyone would take a math class online, but I watched her sit at the table and pretty much teach herself the concepts and pass it. Watching her, I really felt like I married up, and I was so impressed with her dedication and intelligence.

Incidentally, 2001 was the year of the September 11 terrorist attack. I was deep into training for an upcoming air assault school slot. I developed a mental toughness through physical challenges. I felt the most balanced when I pushed myself physically. For six months

I trained for the school by having people drop me off up to fifteen to twenty miles away from the base and ruck back with a forty-five-pound pack. I absolutely loved challenging myself, and it would be a part of me for the remainder of my career. I'll always remember how we found out. My wife was on maternity leave, and I was off as well, so I took our older daughter, Jovana, to school. There was an older Asian lady out in front waving her arms and yelling at everyone that school was closed and to go home and watch the news. I couldn't really understand anything else she was saying because so many people were trying to talk to her at once, so I took our daughter home. My wife and I turned on the TV, and I remember just sitting there in silent sock, wondering if it was some sort of accident. Then I got recalled to head up security at the gates leading to the base. I worked for three weeks straight because of tightened security, even in a place as far away from New York as northern Alaska. As it turned out, it would not be the last time a terrorist incident forced me to step up to a challenge.

A few months following the September 11 attacks, the base leadership showed up to our squadron, and we were all in formation. A staff sergeant was called out of formation, and it was announced that he was being immediately promoted to technical sergeant E6 for his outstanding performance following September 11. What was weird, though, was that he was being lauded for what I had accomplished while leading security at the gates. Although I was not chasing promotion, I knew this situation was not right. This was the same leadership that had awarded me the number one rating of all E5s and the honor of being their noncommissioned officer of the year twice, so *Why not me?*

My wife finished her degree and got accepted to officer training school. She was scheduled to leave in about seven or eight months. Meanwhile, I was convinced that I would be getting out of the air force. When she graduated from OTS, I would have about thirteen months left. I did not reenlist. I liked the idea of social work and giving back. I had developed an interest in learning, and I wanted to share that passion with others by becoming a teacher. There was this program called Troops to Teachers, and I said that when I got out of the air force and finished my degree, I was going to do that. My wife would be an officer, and I would be a teacher. In terms of financially planning for our family, that would be okay. If I made $27,000 annually as a teacher, that would be fine because my wife would be getting the salary of an air force officer.

Meanwhile, I was not even thinking about chasing promotions anymore. At this point, we had a one-year-old and a six-year-old. We were going to send our kids to my mom for the summer, with plans to go to Washington State after my wife finished the twelve-week OTS program in Montgomery, Alabama, where I had once been stationed.

I headed back to Alaska to pack up our stuff and to sell one of our cars. I was going to stay with a friend and then head out, but then my wife called me and said the plans had changed. She wasn't going to Washington; we were going to Japan instead. At this point, I had one year left in the air force. I couldn't go with her to Japan without either extending my time in the air force for two more years or reenlisting entirely.

Staying in Alaska while she went to Japan with our two young kids—and the responsibilities of an officer—did not seem like the best option. I hadn't studied for promotion in two years, because I thought I was getting out of the air force to become a teacher. I had one year left of school. Science and math were circled in red on my degree plan, and I was committed to graduating. I had it all mapped out: I would take those classes in Washington. But now her assignment to Japan put me in a dilemma. In the end, I chose to extend my time in the air force and join her in Japan. Meanwhile, my wife graduated OTS as a second lieutenant.

9

If you want a thing done well, do it yourself.
—Napoleon Bonaparte

MY WIFE AND I TOOK the whole band to Japan and arrived at Yokota Air Base, thirty miles outside of Tokyo. I was a staff sergeant in security forces, and she was a second lieutenant in logistics. About six months after arriving on base, I was hired as a security forces investigator, which was a real turning point in my career. I was sent to an intensive two-month investigations program and hostage negotiations school. I became one of three plainclothes officers. Never in my wildest dreams did I imagine I would excel as a cop. I no longer had issues with being in law enforcement. Rather, I used my past experiences to influence my decision-making as a law enforcement officer.

There was a very diverse squadron at Yokota. I saw people I knew in England and even from tech school. The majority of people in leadership were minorities, and it once again made me feel like the air force was full of great opportunities. But my plan was still to separate from the air force in three years. I was an E5 NCO pursuing the education program, which incidentally happened to be better in Japan. I was still facing those daunting two classes: science and math. Those classes were my biggest hurdles—I had already failed algebra twice.

I signed up for college algebra again. I went out and got all the resources I could, like *College Algebra for Dummies* and instructional DVDs. But I failed the course again and had to pay back $700. I was depressed. I was so close to getting my degree. I shelved math for the time being.

Two months later, I signed up for a science class through the University of Maryland. It was earth science, which I actually found interesting. I happened to be in that science class when I found out I was going to be promoted. One day a friend was passing by my class and called out, "Did you hear about the promotions? You got promoted to E6, technical sergeant." I wasn't even trying to get promoted, and it happened so soon after getting to Japan. But I still wasn't committed to being a lifer. I was excited for the promotion because it meant more money, and I would have an opportunity to be in charge of the investigation sections, which was one of the most coveted jobs in the squadron.

I finished earth science, but I still had to tackle math. I was having anxiety attacks about it. I would go to sign up, but I couldn't do it. Completing algebra would give me two degrees: a BS in human services and an AA in criminal justice in the air force. I was looking at this degree as potentially the biggest accomplishment of my life. I knew I had to get through algebra somehow, so I put out an ad for a tutor. A C130 navigator responded—Yokota was a C130 base—and said he could tutor me. We would meet at the community center. Boy, did I feel small at those meetings. There I was, getting tutored in high school math. I was so frustrated.

Eventually, I started getting the concepts. I met another helpful person one day in the orderly room, a younger NCO. She happened to become a chief master sergeant, E9, years later. We got to talking about this algebra class, which incidentally she needed to take as well. So she took the math class that same semester, and we helped each other through it. I made it out with a B. What I learned through it all, and what became one of my biggest takeaways from that experience, was that perseverance was the key to success.

Three years into our stay in Japan, we both got orders for deployment. My wife was deployed to Iraq, and I was deployed to the Kyrgyz Republic. In Kyrgyzstan, I was in charge of flyaway security and training. I was responsible for protecting a dozen C130s, and I was the personal protection officer for the commander. When he went to the embassy or attended parties with dignitaries, I would step into a nice suit. I acted as his bodyguard in an around areas he had to transit off base and coordinated with his driver whenever he was on the go.

As for my wife, she was headed to Iraq. It was 2005—

the height of the Iraq War—and the country was just gearing up for its first post-Saddam elections. My wife was put in charge of the night shift at Baghdad International Airport, unloading cargo and supervising flight line operations. It was a great opportunity for a relatively new lieutenant. Meanwhile, our kids went back to the States without their parents for the third time in the last few years, which was why we talked about one of us becoming a civilian. As we both were progressing in our military careers, it became more difficult for us to keep the family in a stable environment.

My wife's deployment period overlapped my own. I would come home after seven months, and then she would come home three months later. It would be a year before seeing each other because she had to take the kids to South Carolina before we deployed. We made the best of it. We talked on the phone. But the entire time I knew something was wrong, even though I could not put my finger on it.

Finally, my deployment was over. I was home by myself. Once my wife was home, the plan was to get reacclimated with each other before getting our kids from South Carolina. My oldest daughter was in school, so we didn't want to disrupt that. We thought it would be better for us to wait until we were both home before getting our kids and to wait for our older daughter's school year to be over so our family wouldn't have to face multiple disruptions and reintegration.

Meanwhile, I was still on the path to entering civilian life. I didn't hate being in the air force. I loved what I was doing, but I wanted to teach. I was going to go into the air force reserves or national guard. My wife was trying to decide where she wanted to go in her career. She had just returned from a very tough deployment, and more were on the horizon because of her unique skill set. She was no longer in the squadron, but she had become an executive officer at the group level. It seemed like she was getting her mojo back. I had a date to go to NCO academy in Okinawa at Kadena Air Base. I had about a year left in the air force. This time I was not reenlisting or extending my time. As a family, we were committed to our plan, and we talked about returning to the United States after our tour in Japan.

Around this time, my wife and I were reading books about money and financial planning like *Rich Dad, Poor Dad* and others by the likes of Dave Ramsey and Suzy Orman. Both my wife and I had been raised in homes where the parents worked hard to make ends meet. There had never been discussions of life insurance, mutual funds, investing, or long-term strategic wealth building. We didn't have basic financial literacy growing up. The air force was the first time we heard older people talking about mutual funds and the stock market, and at first it was like it was a foreign language—at least until we started reading these books.

The first time my wife and I saved a thousand dollars, it was so momentous. I even remember where we were. It felt like the biggest accomplishment ever. We were E5 staff sergeants, and before that we would spend our entire salary on unnecessary things. We ate out, bought clothes, and spent money because we had it. The idea of an emergency fund didn't exist to us. In Alaska, we had started putting away money to invest it. That investment in our financial education paid off generationally, as our children were better equipped to navigate the world of finances. My oldest daughter is an accountant, and our youngest daughter opened a mutual fund as soon as she went off to college. As a kid, my mom would drive me around some of the more middle-class neighborhoods to look at the Christmas lights. I always had a fascination with how people earned their place in society. Yes, hard work can help you achieve your goals, but without intellectual literacy, financial literacy, and the ability to look up and see yourself, it will be very difficult to achieve anything.

My date to head off to the NCO academy in Okinawa arrived. Something clicked in me during that time. I suddenly had more motivation to achieve. I think it was the reception I received in my flight room at the school. I had no intention but to do the work and graduate, but I remember what happened at Eielson, where someone less deserving was promoted over me with my accomplishments. This was a *Why not me?* moment, and one I was completely prepared for this time. I thought to myself, *I can communicate well; I'm a natural leader.* The highest awards one can win for leadership in the air force are the John L. Levitow Award for leadership and the Commandant Award for leadership. The Commandant Award is based on a peer vote for leadership. The JLL Award is for leadership and academic performance. It wasn't really my intention to win either of those awards. I knew I had the scores to be a distinguished graduate, but I still didn't think I'd win them. I actually told the commandant that the school needed more discipline and physical training. I thought I offended him. As it turned out, I walked away from the NCO academy with both awards. It was—and still is—extremely rare to win both at the same school. The lesson: never perform less than your capabilities.

While I was at the NCO academy, my wife called. She decided to separate from the air force. She told me there was a program that had been set up because they were trying to downsize their count of officers, and it would help her get out of the air force in sixty days. I knew what she had been through, and I fully supported her decision. But we had always been in the military together. What would happen if we both left? What would that look like? I couldn't picture it financially. The plan had been that my wife would stay in the air force, and I would become a teacher. I had already started working on my MA, since I had those two extra years, and the military would pay for it. We would lose around 65 percent of our income if she got out and relied on my E6 income alone.

I knew I had to make a smart decision, not just in terms of my own career aspirations, but in terms of supporting my family. That's when I committed to the air force as a lifer. I had already been in over nine years, and my family was not ready to be a fully civilian family in terms of income. My older daughter had asthma, my wife was getting great medical care, and both of them had extra medical expenses because of those issues. So I reenlisted. I said to myself, *Okay, I'm good with doing this another ten years. I can teach later.* That day I committed to a career, and my mindset changed completely. I was all in!

My wife was now a civilian, and I was still progressing in the air force. We were still in Japan. She became a government service employee in logistics for the air force. My wife was rebuilding her resiliency after her experiences in Iraq and on returning to Japan. She got heavily involved in yoga. This was in 2005, before it became so culturally popular, which gave her some resilience. Today my wife is a respected yoga teacher, a master trainer, and has taught yoga everywhere, like Costa Rica, Japan, and England. Yoga has been her mechanism for coping and healing—something that has channeled her energy and given her purpose.

For the first time ever, I felt like my life's path was clearly set out before me. I was working investigations as a plainclothes officer. We had been in Japan for four years. After my wife separated from the air force, I felt like we needed some extra income. I was always willing to do what was right or needed in terms of making it happen—a trait that I definitely learned from my mother. In Alaska, I had taken a second job running the skate park in the summertime. In the winter, they asked me if I wanted to work at the rec center, and I drove kids around to the movies. But it was hard to get a second job outside the military in Japan due to the language barrier. On-base jobs were scarce in terms of second job opportunities. They were positions like delivering for Pizza Hut—and even those jobs were scarce because family members of service members often took those jobs. And yet there we were, about to lose half of our income, so I felt like I had to find something.

I was enrolled in my MA classes. One day, I was headed down to the base education office to get some school-related paperwork when I saw a flyer advertising that Central Texas College was looking to hire an adjunct professor of criminal justice. It caught my attention, but I figured there was no way they would hire me. The women working in the office had different ideas. She knew me and kind of pushed the idea on me by giving me a packet to fill out for the position. The application asked applicants to list all their experience. I had taken so many training seminars for criminal justice as part of my job in security. I started writing down a long list of seminars and certifications and qualifications. But I still thought there was no way I could get that job.

Two weeks later, I was in the office again. The school rep told me only two people had put in for this job; the other one was a colonel at headquarters. I was a technical sergeant, so I figured that was the end of my application. Just a short time later, she called me up to stop in the office, which happened to be across the street from where I worked. When I entered the office, she was smiling and told me I had been hired. It was an in-residence position, which meant I would be teaching two nights a week. My first class was twenty-seven students, and I had no idea what to do. I had read books about criminal justice. I had taken classes. I had real-life experience. But there I was, teaching a class—someone who had just barely graduated high school. Although nobody knew my story, I knew I had to get better at teaching. This was another turning point in building the callous mindset that David Goggins later highlights in his bestselling book *Can't Hurt Me* that would be the groundwork for the next decade of my career. This was the foundation of the question, *Why not me!*

The University of Maryland had professors teaching for decades over in Japan. I went into their classes and watched how they taught. I learned about how they developed curriculum. I copied what they were doing, and learning the ropes of how to teach was a crucial step in launching my career as a teacher. Since then, I've taught thousands of students about homeland security and criminal justice over the last sixteen years. But I would have never continued to take a chance on teaching if I hadn't developed a background in education by learning from the best.

I completed my MA and started getting hired at better and better schools. We spent the next few years in Japan. At that time I was an E6, but eighteen months later I was testing for E7. Now that I was committed to the air force, I decided that I was going to give it 100 percent. I was now in charge of security forces training for 140 airmen, which went hand in hand with my off-duty teaching in criminal justice. It was all growing in a positive cycle. My professorship was helping me train the airmen on the job, and my training was helping me teach better in the classroom.

My chief asked if I knew about the FBI National Academy. He told me that he had applied a few times but had never gotten in. They always invited one person from the air force to attend, along with one person from every other branch of the service: navy, army, and the marines. The FBI National Academy was created in 1935 by J. Edgar Hoover and has remained a premier school. All sorts of police agencies across the country send their top talent there. Attendees often become police chiefs in their departments. This was an incredible opportunity, and my chief said he thought I could get in. I said no way. He emphasized that the regulations said applicants must hold a minimum rank of E6, which I was at the time. I asked if they ever admitted any E6s. The answer was no. Typically, applicants had to be at least a master sergeant to get in, and they usually only selected officers.

This where the question of *Why not me?* came into play again. Only this time, it was someone else asking, "Why not you?" He reminded me that I was actively teaching criminal justice and law enforcement in college and on the job. This particular chief outranked me, but he pointed out that even *he* would come to me to learn how to teach. This chief would engage in some real talk with me, telling me that I had to work harder to achieve my goals. But in my case, he pointed out, my self-perception might have been a little off. I was already more than good enough. And that's true for many of us. We think we need to be better than we are, when we're already more than good enough. So again, he put the question to me: Why not you?

The application was daunting. I saw that it required a thorough background check. I didn't want that, even though I had no criminal record. I just didn't want anyone digging into my past. But my chief just kept bringing me into his office and asking me over and over again to apply. So, I put the application together. I had to get a letter of approval from my senior master Sergeant, and this fellow was a lot more skeptical than the chief about my ability to get into the program. But he gave me the letter.

I took it to my captain, and he said, "No way, you're

not going for that." He and I had recurring issues over the past three years. He was a mixed-race fellow, but there was no camaraderie over that point for us. He seemed to have a vendetta against me. He had no MA. He was prior enlisted, now an officer, so if I corrected him on anything, it created some tension. As it turned out, he was also applying to attend the FBI National Academy, so there was this weird competition between us. Really, there shouldn't have been, because there was no maximum number of people who could be nominated. I told him the chief and the commander wanted to nominate me. He could be nominated as well—no problem.

To make a long story short, the chief said the captain was wrong about me and that my package was going up through the four or five layers it needed to pass through before the final decision. I then had to go through background checks and security checks by the FBI—the whole thing took around a year. Meanwhile, I made it to E7. The first time out of the gate, I passed the test and was a master sergeant. Just four years before that I was in Japan as an uncommitted E5, just wanting to finish my BS and get out of the air force. I was tired of people telling me no or putting barriers in my way. My callous mindset grew harder, and I refused to be treated like I was less than anyone else ever again. Either outwork me, or get out of my way.

One day we were at morning PT, lined up in a circle like we always were. Someone would step in the middle and lead PT for the day. We started doing the exercises. Then my commander came into the middle of the circle. No official message had come out yet. But he told me—in front of everybody—that I had been selected. It was a real *Why not me?* moment. I was headed to the FBI National Academy, and the captain wasn't. I was the FBI selection for the air force and first E6 selection ever. There hasn't been one since.

By that point, I had been in the air force for twelve years. Learning about my selection validated all the hard work I had put into improving myself—driving home practically crying that I couldn't learn high school math and the late nights spent correcting the blotters soaked in red ink. I felt like I could accomplish anything.

It takes about a year from selection to attendance before candidates actually enter the FBI National Academy. Every class is set up to be credited as a BA or a MA. When I arrived, I picked my track and thoroughly enjoyed the twelve-week program in Quantico, Virginia. I was surrounded by professionals in law enforcement from around the country. I had even seen some of them on TV, like the spokesperson for the LAPD. Other notables included the head of inspectors of the Philadelphia Police Department, head of security for the sultan of Brunei, and the head of security for the city of Mecca.

Graduates of this program went on to be important people in corporate security and public law enforcement. It was an amazing opportunity. There I was, taking classes and eating dinner with future police colonels and the head of the Boston bomb squad. I didn't know if I was worthy, but I completed the program. At the end of the course, I graduated with a 3.9 GPA. For me, graduating from the program was the culmination of so much hard work to improve myself. I had failed the fourth grade. I had dropped out of high school. I had failed my ASVAB the first time around, and I barely made it into the air force on the second try. Now I was turning in twenty-five-page papers and learning with the most decorated law enforcement personnel in the world. Twelve years earlier, I was a moment away from being a felon and not graduating from high school. Now I was standing on a stage with the attorney general of the Unites States and the director of the FBI, graduating from the one of the prestigious law enforcement institutions in the world.

Graduation Day at the FBI Academy

After the program, I headed back to Japan. Our family was coming up on its sixth year there. I went back to that napkin. "When you are mature enough, go to Korea."

One of the ways to merit the privilege of going overseas was to take a short tour for one year, and then I could choose my next assignment. I was an E7, mature, married, and not really into partying anymore. I put in for Korea and found out I was going. I had a new chief who was equally supportive and is still a friend of mine today. He turned out to be a phenomenal leader. The trip I volunteered to take before Korea was going to be a special deployment for four to five months. He wouldn't tell me where it was or what it was exactly, but he told me that he needed a strong leader for the group. Otherwise, he wouldn't feel comfortable. He wanted to know I was committed before telling me the location. I talked it over with my wife, and she was okay with it. The chief made sure I understood that it was a volunteer opportunity and that he wasn't forcing me. I said I was in.

This special deployment ended up being to the Caribbean island of Curacao. It was a counterdrug mission of twenty-seven people. Curacao was a resort island, and we had a lot of downtime. We stayed in a resort beachfront casino as we secured a small installation. My wife actually came out to visit me for one week. This deployment ended up being a much-needed break. After I had committed to the air force, I started firing on all cylinders to make up for what I thought was lost time in terms of career growth. But I had been burning myself out.

On returning to Japan, I had about three months to go before heading off to Korea. One of the main reasons I was also interested in going to Korea at that point was because my family was still in Japan. They were only an hour flight away. Airmen with family back in the United States would only get to see them midtour, but I could see mine almost any time.

I got a phone call from the security forces operations

commander in Korea. He knew that I graduated from the FBI National Academy and had a strong background in investigations. I was told that I would be helping combat human trafficking and drugs, and I should bring my civilian clothes. I had been thinking I was going to be a flight chief. Instead, I was going to run a task force to identify trends in human trafficking. My position was to be the chief of intelligence and task force leader to reduce human trafficking and illicit drug sales, a dual position that did not yet exist. The task force didn't even exist yet either. I was going to have to bring it together with some investigators, a town patrol of around fifteen people to go around at night, four US investigators, two local Korean investigators, a liaison from the Korean National Police, and a force protection office of two people to do intel. Also, while in Korea, I was charged with starting up a hostage negotiations team. As the only certified negotiator on the base, I put together a small five-person team. This would prove to be a critical decision—one that would save lives. Not a month after the team was assembled, we were recalled to an individual who had taken a weapon from the armory and may have been homicidal and suicidal. Today my leadership company teaches empathy and connection as our signature course. That decision is largely from the results of these incidents. When the team assembled, initial reports were that the individual illegally removed a pistol and thirty rounds of ammunition from the armory and was potentially looking for his wife. He was having marital issues, and we had no idea what his intentions were or where he was headed. We eventually found his wife and ensured she was safe. Just five days before this incident, this same individual showed up to my office and wanted to report that his spouse was cheating on him. Our office did not handle these types of complaints, and we referred him to the first sergeant. Prior to him leaving, my female investigator asked if he wanted to smoke a cigarette. She listened to him for over an hour, and my senior investigator, Sal, also spoke to him. They showed empathy and connected with him. The night of the incident, I was the only negotiator with any experience talking to anyone in crisis. I made the decision to make the female investigator the primary, since she had built trust with him. It was a very long night. The negotiations lasted over five hours. He fired a round during the stand-off. We thought he had taken his own life. Eventually, she was able to convince him to turn himself in. The one lesson was the same lesson I had learned after walking out of that phone booth in 1995: building relationships based on empathy and connection can save lives. It was a turning point in all our lives, and it set the tone for how we handled the biggest challenge of the assignment, which was combatting human trafficking.

These clubs were off base in Korea proper. The scene has really changed today, but back then there were around 120 clubs to entertain service members with girls from Russia or the Philippines, mostly working there against their will. These clubs would lure girls into Korea with the glamor of signing entertainment contracts. When they got to Korea, they would be put to work serving expensive drinks and paying their way out of what was essentially indentured servitude. If they didn't sell enough drinks, they could get out of debt by renting themselves out for the night or any number of other thinly veiled paths to prostitution. Many of them had their passports taken away. They were helpless and couldn't get home. Our job was to crack down on all this and prevent service members from going to these places—not necessarily by shutting them down but by removing their clientele. On the surface, these things seem harmless. To this day, a few of my team members and I still discuss this time in our lives. I met several young girls who we got know to include their stories. I remember one particular story about "Maria," who told us how she signed an entertainment contract with the hopes of being hired to sing. Once she arrived, she was placed in a small apartment with at least ten other girls, and her passport was taken. Once she realized she wasn't going to be singing, she was slowly groomed into selling drinks and eventually selling her body. These stories became the backdrop of a personal mission to change the system.

Within two or three months, we were already cracking down. If we could prove a place was involved in any human trafficking or holding girls against their will, we would make it off-limits to the military. We couldn't close it down, but if 99 percent of the customers didn't come, they lost their business. We were enforcing good order and discipline, and two or three of the largest clubs closed down. The folks who owned the clubs got upset, of course. This kind of crackdown had been seen before, but with less effectiveness. In the past, clubs might close for a day or two. But this time was different. The culture was different. Human trafficking couldn't be overlooked now, and our military didn't want any dealings with it. It was only a short time before the club owners figured out we were serious. Recordings were left at the gate of the base—meetings about how they were going to handle the task force, talk about harming leaders, and sometimes even veiled death threats. It kind of took me back to high school. There was no paranoia this time—this was real. I felt a sort of reckless fearlessness. I was told not to go off base.

At that point in my life, I didn't want to show that type of fear. I wasn't reckless, but our team was going out and doing so much good work. One of the best investigators I had ever met, Sal, ran the day-to-day investigation ops. He set up a great plan in which everyone had assigned tasks that brought the team together. It was one of the best teams I've ever worked with. Young investigators made great contacts with girls. The Filipino embassy was willing to help the girls get home without a passport. At least a dozen girls who we took out of bad situations went home. It was a challenging year, but a very rewarding year, as we made a difference in people's lives. Our task force even won an award for the work we did against human trafficking. Most people had no idea of the level of work we were involved in. We ran counternarcotic operations targeting low-level drugs sales to military personnel. I would be dishonest if I did not acknowledge that my prior knowledge of the drug game came in handy. The drug game is fueled by greed, and that's what we capitalized on. One particular operation involved a Russian female who was operating in the nightclub district offering several narcotics. She was an attractive, mid-twenties female who was skilled at luring in service members. She represented a threat on several fronts. One of my young investigators befriended her, and after a few weeks, we convinced her of a party happening on base with transiting military personnel who were looking for drugs. We partnered with the Korean National Police, and she came on to the base with a bag of drugs. We removed a clear threat, and it was one of our brightest moments.

When I was in Bosnia and involved with running humanitarian convoys, I was younger and hadn't appreciated the scope of the operation. Now I had kids of my own, I was older, and I saw the effects of what we were doing. I remember how exhausted we were and the emotional toll this took on us. The human trafficking, where the girls were forced to live—we knew the backstory behind the flashy lights in front of the club. We actually felt like we had just scratched the surface with our work, but so much has changed for the positive there. We knew we didn't stop human trafficking around the world, but we sure put a dent in it wherever we were sent.

10

Tough times never last, but tough people do.
—Robert H. Schuller

I LEFT KOREA AS A master sergeant, E7. I did not get promoted to senior master sergeant, E8, and I was devastated about it. My mindset had changed from the days when I did not remove the study material from its package. I was invested and wanted to excel. My performance evaluation was due, and because I was in such a nontraditional position that did not make many friends, I was not sure what would happen. The commander gave me high recommendations for my next promotion. We had record numbers in terms of reducing human trafficking and drug busts in Korea, with over 340 violations flagged. We put a serious dent in the bad culture we had been trying to get rid of, and it kicked off a campaign of fighting back against illicit activities, which are almost nonexistent in that area today.

I picked up my family in Japan, and we headed back to RAF Lakenheath, the location of my first overseas assignment. I was so fascinated by Europe that I wanted to go back to England for another assignment. But this time, fourteen years later, we were headed back with two kids, and I was in a leadership position as a flight chief in charge of seventy-five people. Before I left Korea, I had been told I would be working logistics at Lakenheath—taking care of vehicles, weapons, equipment, and conducting weapons training.

When I arrived in Lakenheath, there was a new chief there. I came in and reported to the squadron. The tradition was that an SNCO reports to the chief, and when I did, I was surprised and elated to see that the chief was also an African American. I had worked for two other Black chiefs in the previous fourteen years. Based on my previous experiences, I felt he would be more relatable and could provide some mentorship toward my career progression. Boy, was I wrong about that.

I walked in and introduced myself. Right away he said, "I know who you are."

I was thrown off. I said, "Okay . . ." and went on introducing myself. I was coming in from Korea and would be in charge of logistics—at least, that's what my sponsor had told me. This chief said that wouldn't be happening, or in his words, "No, you're not."

I replied, "Oh, okay, sir. That's just what I was told before I got here."

He told me I was making an ass of myself with that assumption. I thought, *This conversation is not going how I thought it was going to go.* I had never had a conversation like this, not even as a junior airman at the bottom of the totem pole. This chief had never met me. I didn't know what I had been doing to offend him, and I didn't know why this conversation was going south.

He gave me a tone and told me I was going to a flight where I'd be in charge of security. Being a flight chief was an honorable charge. Flight chiefs got to be influential leaders with younger airmen. I actually had been hoping to be a flight chief in Korea, but because of my special skills in investigations, they put me in charge of special investigations. I had been a flight chief as a technical sergeant, E6, and enjoyed it. So I didn't understand the condescension in his tone. "You're not going to come in here and be in charge of logistics."

What was that all about?

Whatever the case was, he did not want me going into logistics, and that was clear. So, my response to this news was a feeling of being honored, despite whatever was going on with him—and I shared that. Well, he kept on going with it, asking me if I was being a smart-ass.

I said, "No, I love being a flight chief." Flight chief only goes up to master sergeant. After E7, you generally can't be a flight chief anymore in security forces, so this was potentially my last chance to be one. Despite the fact that I wasn't expecting this exchange, I viewed this as a favor. If I had entered logistics and made it to E8, I wouldn't get to be a flight chief ever again. But even so, the conversation was uncomfortably confrontational.

In any case, I went to flight and had seventy-five airmen under my charge. It was an amazing time. This was about four to five months before E8 promotions would be announced. In the meantime, this chief would come through the gate and find fault with everyone under my charge, calling me up and yelling at me. It disturbed me. Truth be told, there shouldn't be any favoritism between people of the same race, but I still felt that as a younger Black man, he should be mentoring me, and he wasn't.

Fast-forward a few months, and my flight was the best flight in the squadron. The most professional, the highest morale, and the best qualifications. We had the best time rates for administrative work. I had learned how to lead in this way from Sergeant Dixon, who ran a tight ship concerning discipline. Whenever there was an exercise, inspection, or showcase, they wanted my flight to do it. Out of twenty-seven master sergeants under the charge of this chief, I was probably one of the youngest. I had good records and public accolades from Korea. I was in the newspaper for cases involving hostage negotiations. Korea was a good year for me. I think that all bothered this chief.

Security Force Flight

The E8 results came out. We couldn't see our scores right away, but the highest possible score was 450. Promotions usually came at a cutoff of 370–380. When I had tested before, I got around a 370 and did not make it. These scores were compiled by board members who scrutinized ten years of each applicant's military career.

I was notified that I made it. The chief had his favorites, and I was not one of them. He would place his favorites in promotable positions, but their records were not half as good as others. I always told people to control their immediate situations. Even though from day one this chief tried to slow me down, I never let him discourage me. I never stopped being the person I thought I could be in my leadership position. I never spoke poorly about him; I just focused on leading.

There was one other person from our squadron on the promotion list—a White female he also did not like. We were the only two out of twenty-seven master sergeants under his charge who got promoted. I think it shocked him that we were the two who made it because we were the only two he did not mentor. I think this rubbed him the wrong way—we made it without him.

Two days after the list came out, we could pull out our score notices. I didn't really care what it was, but I did not intend to communicate whatever it was to the chief. Mine was a 442.5, which meant that two people on the panel saw my service as meriting a perfect 10, and the other a 9.5. Although we couldn't see other people's scores, we could look online to see the board groupings—that is, how many people got each score. The group scores showed that nobody out of a thousand people around the world got a perfect score. Only *one* person got a 442.5, and that was me. I was the one person in the entire security forces career field. That meant I had the number one board score for security forces master sergeants, which meant that the panel thought my work was the best.

I could not believe it, because I always heavily scrutinized myself, no matter how many accolades I got. So I *definitely did* show that score to the chief. He looked at it and looked at me in disbelief. When I had first met him, he told me that people were calling him telling him how hot I was for promotion, but he had read my records and felt that I wasn't. But there he was, looking at concrete numbers showing I was the best master sergeant in all security forces out of a few thousand people who had tested. And I don't think he liked it, either.

This ongoing experience really left me floored. Another Black man in the *same job* as me. Why did he hate me? I could not understand it. Was it that he wanted to be the only Black person excelling in the air force? He was a chief master sergeant. He had a MA. His office was full of accolades. He'd been in the air force for twelve or thirteen years longer than I had, and he had a decent run. I was young but had also been in the service for fourteen years. I could replace him in his position one day when he retired. So why didn't he want to help me out? Back in Yokota, my superior, Chief White, did everything to make sure I excelled. He's the reason why I started my MA before I even got my BS diploma in the mail. Another chief, Chief Peters, believed in me and gave me opportunities. But here was a man who *looked like me* who was doing more against me than anyone who had covertly or overtly discriminated against me. This took me back to the hallways at Maxwell thirteen years earlier, when I overheard three men plotting against three Black airmen. But this time, I was different. I had a callus mindset, and I asked, "Why not me?" from a place of strength. I forced people to see me, hear me, and value me.

There were only two positions available to E8s, and one of them was logistics. This chief had an E7 in there. When I got promoted, I was on flight. After all the run-around, I was going to get switched to logistics after all. I didn't want to antagonize the chief over this. The promotion came in March. Before I knew it, it was May, and I was doing some routine paperwork in the office. The commander saw me. He was a great guy who took a helpful interest in me. He was surprised to see me and asked me what I was doing. Later on, this same commander pulled me out of some dark moments in the aftermath of a terrorist incident by sending me to Qatar for a year. Anyway, he saw me in the office filling out this paperwork, with my weapons and gear on, which I would not have been wearing if I was working logistics. I told him I was about to go to work. He asked me if I was still on flight, and I replied in the affirmative. He stared at me for maybe forty seconds before going back to his business.

I would later learn the commander and the chief did not have a good relationship. I didn't see a lot of the interactions between people at HQ, because my shift started at 10:00 p.m., but that was one thing I found out. A few days later, I got a call from the flight commander, who said I was going to logistics to be the superintendent on Monday, where I would be in charge of ammunition, equipment, weapons, and training thousands of airmen. This squadron was one of the most heavily deployed squadrons in the air force, and my job would be to train and deploy, which was why they needed an E8. I was going to be teamed up with a Black captain I had mentored when he was a lieutenant, so I was excited to be joining the team. But before he got there, I was in charge for about forty-five days.

The antagonistic chief would come over a lot. One day he asked me if I wanted to go to lunch. I was thrown off. Well, lunch was awkward. As I found out, he did not like the commander. He was trying to get me on his team now. I was in charge of resources for the squadron, and the resource advisors, who oversaw the finances and procurement, worked for me. I didn't control the money, but I made sure everything was purchased and briefed the commander about it. This chief wanted me to bring him any kind of financial reporting before I took it to the commander and also make purchases authorized by him. In my mind, I was not going to do that. I didn't say anything though. This was the guy who had done nothing for anyone, and I saw a second gear of this person on top of that. After lunch, I went about my business.

Fast-forward about a month. The chief was about to deploy for six months. The way the ranking structure worked, I was waiting to put on my E8, but I would move up into E8 Operations Superintendent position in his absence. The current E8 operations superintendent would take the chief's place, but then he got deployed too. In the end, I would level up by two spots. I was excited to be an operations superintendent, which meant

I would be in charge of all flight chiefs. That meant I would be bumped into the chief's spot while he was deployed. I could see the pain on his face telling me about this situation.

I was the senior enlisted leader and a few months away from putting on E8. The master sergeants were used to being led by a chief, but now someone with the same number of stripes was leading them. I was good at building teams and didn't make it about me. The chief had created some bad energy in the squadron. People were nervous around him.

March 1, 2011, I finally got to put on senior master sergeant, E8. I had waited a whole year to put this on after getting my promotion announced. I was in charge of a 430-person squadron. I was surrounded by great mentors in charge of other squadrons. These mentors would answer my question and make sure I had the tools I needed. When I put on that E8, I breathed a sigh of relief. It wasn't that I needed the stripe to lead, but now I could focus on other things without worrying that I didn't have the stripes to match my leadership position.

One day later, on March 2, we were going to have a visit from senior air force leadership and deploy some teams. Every time we would send out a team, we would have a send-off at the dormitory. Family would be there saying goodbye. The commander and the chief would give a speech on the bus after they said their goodbyes. It was always a proud moment, wishing them well. This particular team was led by two young staff sergeants. That morning started like so many others when we would depart our teams. I remember speaking to all the spouses there and the kids and being the last person on the bus before they took off. I told the team leaders it was their time to lead and that I was proud of them. “Do not worry about things back here. We will take care of your families.” I had been on both sides of this type of send-off. When I deployed, my wife was there in the family crowd, and when my wife deployed, I was there in the family crowd. So I knew the emotions going all around. Since I was also in charge of putting on a visit from a senior leader later on, I was running around with a technical sergeant all day setting it up and making sure the stage was there. That’s when I got the call from the unit deployment manager: “Our guys got shot.”

I’ll never forget those words. We had over 100 people deployed all over the world, some of them in hot spots like Afghanistan. *Was our team engaged in combat?* That was my first thought.

No, it was the team that just left. They had been in Frankfurt International Airport. They were going to be training and then heading to their location. I stopped in my tracks, trying to register what I was being told. The unit deployment manager was on the phone with one of the staff sergeant leaders there. We were hearing reports that a lot of them had been injured or killed. For Germany, this was similar to September 11.

At this point, I was a senior master sergeant who had that stripe on for just twenty-four hours. There was no phone-a-friend in a moment like that. The commander, who was a great leader and a lieutenant colonel, was on a cruise with his wife in the Mediterranean. So we had a young captain as our acting commander. All the bells and alarms started going off. This terrorist attack was getting coverage on major networks like CNN. Phones were going off. We were facing the biggest crisis I had ever seen in my service. I was getting calls from HQ, from Germany, from all over. Parents were calling. Spouses were calling. Everybody wanted to know what was going on.

We were trying to sort through the entire ordeal. We were in England while they were in Germany. The initial reports were worse than what ended up occurring. We were trying to sort through that information. About two hours into it, we were told about one casualty: Senior Airman Nicholas Alden. I remember a sinking feeling. All of us stood there and took that news like a punch to the gut. We looked around for about ten seconds. We just saw his wife and two young kids say goodbye to him. We were told other airmen were badly injured. The bus driver who was assigned to the bus was also killed.

For about twenty-seven straight hours, we did not sleep. I did not go home. As this happened, my sister and her husband were flying to visit me. I had relatives in midair. With the terrorist attack in Germany, they were stopping the movement of all military people as they tried to figure out whether this was a solitary attack or a wide-ranging threat. It was a haywire day. My young captain had to put on his service dress uniform and notify a spouse that her husband was dead. We had people in Germany we couldn't contact. Authorities there had sequestered the team. We had airmen in the ICU who possibly wouldn't survive, and we were trying to get their spouses over to Germany to see them, and I was orchestrating all of this. This was where the team responded. The captain stood up that day.

Master sergeants were stepping up. I said to one of them, "Hey, you, pack up your bags and make sure we're there for them." I said to another SNCO, "Hey, you, go with this spouse to Germany and make sure she can see her husband." Everyone in the squadron stepped up to take care of each other.

We recalled the entire squadron. The incident was all over the news already, but we wanted to get the most accurate information out to the squadron. We called three hundred or so people into the gym. It was an emotional moment, and people were crying. A four-star general had flown in from Germany to address our squadron. But that wasn't what really moved me. What moved me was that after he spoke, he stood in the door and shook hands and hugged more than 300 people as they filed by him. It wasn't just a gesture of being there for us but an unscripted moment of human connection. Then we were back in a twenty-seven-hour marathon. But the general didn't leave our side. It was needed that night, and it gave us strength.

The cruise ship our commander was on with his family docked for excursions in Turkey, and he got an immediate flight back to England. From the time of the incident, it took him two days to get to us, but he jumped right in. He and I got on a plane and went to Germany to visit the bedsides of our airmen in the hospital, some of them still sedated. I remember when one of them woke up and saw us at the end of the bed. He tried to get up and show a sign of respect. He had been shot three times, so, of course, we made him lie down. But that heroic gesture almost broke me inside.

RAF Lakenheath Fallen Defender Memorial

I was seeing in real time the character of these airmen. To this day, I wish more people could see these Americans to appreciate what they give to their country. This airman had been shot in the arm, leaving him with some limited mobility in that limb. When he received the Purple Heart, the general waived away the salute, but he trembled his arm upward to give one anyway. I tell you, there was not a dry eye in the room. To me, that was character. The staff sergeant on the bus had actually been shot through the head. We thought he wasn't going to survive, but he did. He was medically retired from the air force. If he had his way, he probably would have kept serving. To this very day, he still wants to serve no less than anyone in uniform. I still keep in touch with him. He's been a source of inspiration to active service members and in his work with Wounded Warriors.

Thankfully, we got the rest of the airmen back home safely. Unfortunately, they would be affected by post-traumatic stress disorder (PTSD). PTSD can stem from both combat and noncombat situations. These young people were not on a battlefield, but they saw something horrific that caught them by surprise. Someone entered a bus and started shooting at people in close quarters. The only reason more people weren't killed is because the gun jammed, and the second staff sergeant chased him off the bus.

This is where compassion comes into the equation. Despite not having any physical wounds, they were hurting inside. Over the next two years, we had a lot of people dealing with something. It made me look at what was important as a leader: Our people were important. We had to make tough decisions, but they needed to be about our people. Dealing with the fallout of that event created overwhelming twelve-to-fifteen-hour workdays. I was coming home and not worth much to my family.

Three months after the incident, the antagonistic chief returned to base. I had been leading this squadron for six months through this trauma. We had lost airmen, but we built bonds in the squadron out of necessity to bring people closer together. The only thing I was hoping was that the chief would recognize the magnitude of the moment. Petty tactics and favoritism could not be sustained in our organization. We also had people getting back from Afghanistan who were engaged in combat operations. One team had led the defense of Forward Operating Base Fenty, taking out several insurgents and defending the base from a breach. We had lost another airman to an accident right on base, when he was hit by a car.

But the chief was not concerned about me or about the organization. We had started a physical training program for morale with sixty to seventy airmen. The chief didn't believe it was good and was upset about it. We had rearranged the squadron and put pride into it. We beautified the areas around our buildings, and we took care of our people even if they weren't fully operational. Some people couldn't carry a weapon because of their mental health.

I was at a breaking point myself. I wanted help for my mental health, but I felt like the people around me needed me more, and that was a mistake. I was becoming someone unrecognizable to my family, but I was keeping a straight face at work. My commander was on his way out, and the chief was back from his deployment. I was going to go back to my old job in logistics.

When the chief came back, he was on fourteen days of rest and recuperation. But he wasn't married, which meant he spent every day of his break at work. He came into the office and railed against everything. He wasn't concerned about how people were doing. He wanted to make all these changes and return things to the way they were under his watch. I wasn't at a breaking point; I was already broken. I could not take on his baggage, too. I wanted to go back to my old job, and I figured that the new commander would deal with the chief. This was full circle for me. I had so many successes in my career. I had overcome wanting to take my own life, and now I found myself dealing with similar feelings I had at nineteen.

Shortly after the chief returned, I had gotten a phone call from a senior NCO who wanted to talk in person. A staff sergeant deployed with the chief was very concerned because his career had been threatened. Every six months—or a year, depending on their scores—everyone had to take a PT test. This chief happened to be overweight and asked the staff sergeant to input a passing score for him without taking the test. Not just any score—a high score. The staff sergeant did it; then the chief called him on his personal number and told the staff sergeant to meet him. He told him, "I control your career and what you do. If you tell anyone about this, it's over for you."

Well, that staff sergeant finally told someone about it, and they told me. So, on top of everything else, I now had this dilemma in my lap. I was just three days from leaving my job, and I got this huge atomic bomb. But integrity is one of our core values in the air force. This master sergeant was looking at me to make a decision. Who would I be if I just did nothing? A fraud. So I went home and thought about which course of action to take.

I called the captain I had worked with in logistics. Ultimately, I would need to bring it up to the commander. I had a good relationship with the commander. We were together every day, but I just needed some perspective before I brought this up to him. I knew that once I brought this up with the commander, I was taking on the weight of being the one who went up against a chief master sergeant. That could have some consequences. Maybe I would never get promoted again. If the chief didn't get in trouble, I would be through. If he did get in trouble, I might still be labeled by other chiefs as the guy who brought him down. I also talked this over with the chaplain. I was talking to the chaplain about other issues. I had a little bit of guilt over the terrorist incident: Did I make the right decisions about who I chose to deploy? Was it my fault airmen were injured or killed? I signed off on Airman Alden deploying as a replacement, and that decision has haunted me. My marriage was struggling because of all the time I was spending at work. I was still spending fourteen hours a day working, seven of which were just talking to people. It's important to have an outlet for these emotional issues.

I explained the situation to the commander. That day, I resolved that I would retire in a year or two, and it would all be okay. After all, I had made it to E8. The commander needed statements from the staff sergeant, and he wanted me to get them. I asked if someone else could collect the details. I wanted to remain neutral so it didn't look like I was the one driving the train. We assigned a neutral captain from outside the squadron. After a long investigation, the chief was fired and demoted to E8. Now he and I were the same rank. They gave him a job in HQ until he retired a year later. He showed up unannounced to my office one day. I was surprised when I looked up. Honestly, for a brief second, I thought maybe he was there to try to harm me. Even though it had been sixteen years since I left home, my street smarts never left me. I could recognize a threat a mile away. We had a good conversation, and I could tell he had some regrets and shame about the way he acted. I did not take the moment to make him feel small. I felt he probably had some real insecurities in his life to make him act the way he did toward people. I wished him the best and extended my hand. That was the last time we saw or spoke to each other.

But I had one more proverbial last hour. The senior master sergeant was back from Afghanistan, but he had gotten in trouble, too, over a different problem. He didn't lose his stripe, but the commander said he could not replace the chief who had been fired. So I would retain leadership of the squadron, and the senior master sergeant would be second to me, which caused a lot of tension between us.

We got a new commander later that summer, and he was one of the best leaders I'd ever served under. He came in full force and took on the daunting task of getting to know people and their issues. I was still acting as the chief, so a week into the job I went into the commander's office. I told him I was sure he had been briefed on everything that happened there. I'd been doing the job for nine months, and suggested he hire an actual chief to come into the organization and replace me, which seemed like the right thing.

But the commander brushed off my concerns. "Don't worry," he told me. I would be left in a chief position until leaving a year later. Everyone thought I was doing a great job and that it would be better to leave me in charge to avoid disrupting the flow of what was going on. I was honored but terrified at the same time. I knew the state I was in mentally, even if they didn't see it. If it wasn't for the commander and first sergeant, I wouldn't have made it. I was mending my marriage and getting myself back together while leading 430 people. The first sergeant became someone I could lean on and share some vulnerability about my stress. The commander was easy to talk to. Since he was there without his family, he would work late sometimes, so we had a lot of late-night chats at work. He was religious, and I think he could see when I was struggling with something. He had this ability to draw out whatever was bothering me, even if I was reluctant to share it. They were two great wingmen.

The commander and I did everything we could to take care of our people. The German government invited us to come with the staff sergeant who had chased the gunman off the bus and up an escalator to award him the highest medal the German government could bestow on foreign soldiers or civilians. The award ceremony was highly televised. The German defense minister himself pinned the award on the staff sergeant and recognized his efforts to save lives while putting himself at risk.

There was a best squadron award for every career field in the air force, with three levels for small, medium, and large squadrons of over two hundred people. We were a large squadron, and there were other large security force squadrons all over the world. We were submitted for an award when I was acting chief. The last time this squadron had won was in 1987—now it was 2011. We won. It was a proud, validating moment for me as a leader. Just eighteen months earlier, I had been sitting in the previous chief's office, with him saying he didn't want to give me an opportunity.

Everywhere I've been I've had to go through barriers. And now here we were, getting recognition for the whole squadron. I remember thinking to myself, *Why not us?* We deserved this recognition. We ended up winning that award the next year as well. We won this award two years in a row. It was really a testament to the character of our people. They were buying into our guiding principle: treat everyone with dignity and respect. We were led by a passionate commander. I felt like we could not be stopped.

11

Doubt kills more dreams than failure ever will.
—Suzy Kassem

AT THE END OF MY three-year tour in Lakenheath, I was rated number one out of seventy-seven senior master sergeants on base, which meant I had a good chance of making chief master sergeant in the next round of promotions. I hadn't particularly been striving for E9, because there was so much going on—the terrorist incident, the fallout, and the way my work was negatively affecting my marriage.

We had the option of relocating to Los Angeles or space command in Colorado Springs. Those were the only two available positions for a security forces senior master sergeant. This would be the first time in sixteen years we could live in the United States. The last time I was in the States, I had been an E3 at Maxwell Air Force Base. Since then, I had traveled to over thirty countries all over the world—Asia, Europe, and the Middle East—and now I would be returning as a senior master sergeant with a wife and two kids, one of them entering her junior year of high school.

We chose Colorado Springs. I was unfamiliar with Los Angeles, and with a fifteen-year-old going into high school, I could not take the gamble. It turned out to be a great choice for our family. We loved the area and fell in love with the outdoors. As far as work went, nothing exciting went on there for about five months. It was my first time working on headquarters staff—a career-broadening position that allowed me to see things on a big-picture level. It wasn't the most hands-on work; it was mostly policy and paperwork. This was the first time I was in a cubicle all day, in charge of equipment for space command bases and the deployment readiness database. At the same time, I knew that chief master sergeant results were coming out, and if I made it, I'd be leaving the base.

Before I knew it, I was only about five days away from the release of chief master sergeant results. Only 1 percent of the air force were chief master sergeants: that's three thousand people out of three hundred thousand airmen. Chief master sergeant was the highest enlisted rank that one could make, and I had this opportunity coming my way after just eighteen years in the air force. The average time for that promotion was around twenty-two years.

One of the civilian leaders on base was someone who

I had actually worked for in Saudi Arabia when I was at Khobar Towers. He had been a flight chief back then. One day, he asked me if I had heard anything about chief master sergeant results. For three days after that question, I felt so nervous. I was physically ill. A lot of people had faith in me, and I was nervous about whether or not I had passed the test for E9 because I didn't want to disappoint anyone. I was also worn out. Maybe I didn't want to make it to E9 after all. I had been in the air force eighteen years already, and I was thinking that maybe it was time to apply for retirement. Lakenheath had worn me out physically and mentally, but I could never show that. And yet I was depleted on the inside.

For some reason, great things always seemed to happen to me at PT. It was where I got the majority of good news given to me during my time in the air force. One afternoon at PT, my chief gave me the news: I made chief master sergeant. As I drove home, I was so happy about it. I called my wife and my mom, and I was literally crying with joy. It is one of the few times I have cried about something in my life. I don't think it was entirely about the promotion. I think there had just been so many feelings bottled up inside because of my stress with work and the terrorist incident, but there was also something deeper. Just eight years prior to this, I had no intention of even staying in the air force. Since then, I had worked so hard and made a lot of personal sacrifices to get to this point. This promotion to the highest possible enlisted rank just kind of opened up a pressure valve inside of me, and the emotions came pouring out. It was vindicating for me personally, especially thinking about all the barriers I had to break to get there. I called my mom and thanked her. There were so many thoughts running through my mind on that drive home. I was told by my father I would be back in two weeks. I was told in BMT I would not make it to graduation. I was told I was stupid. I was told I would not graduate college. I was told I would never go past master sergeant, E7, and here I was, promoted to the highest enlisted grade in the military four years before the average promotion time. *Why not me?*

Now they had to find a chief master sergeant job for me. As it so happened, there was a position available for security forces squadron chief at the Air Force Academy, right there in Colorado Springs. I interviewed and got the job the next day. The person I would be replacing was actually a good friend of mine from Japan.

We moved across town to the Air Force Academy, but it would be another nine to ten months before I put on chief. My new commander was a female major. She was a fun person to work with, we got along just fine, but our styles were very different. I tried to help her see some of her own blind spots about accountability and giving information over to her boss, the colonel. One day, about five months into the job, we were told she was going to be removed from command. I felt like I hadn't done my job or helped her out enough. Leadership at any level is all in. If you are not willing to tell people the truth regardless of the outcome, maybe leadership is not for you. At this point, over a twenty-year career, I earned a reputation for being brutally honest with leaders regardless of their rank. I did not gain a lot of friends or invites to cocktail parties, but I held those responsible for others' welfare to a standard that ensured we did not take our people and their families for granted. Basically, either you are built for it, or you are not.

Leadership can be a lonely place. It's important to have a strong support system. I was lucky to have two great first sergeants, Steve and Amber, and a great senior master sergeant operations superintendent who could lead with his eyes closed. This all made my job easier and helped the squadron to function efficiently. But I wanted to provide that same type of quality support for my own leadership. If they didn't succeed, I felt partially responsible.

Spartan Race with my Frist Sergeant

This was an additional weight on my back after everything I had gone through at Lakenheath in the aftermath of the terrorist incident. I felt so much pressure, but I didn't feel like I had anyone I could talk to. I didn't want to burden my wife, since Lakenheath had already caused so many problems in our marriage. So I went back to the chaplain to seek some mental health counseling. At this point, I was in my mid-thirties. I was more mature and willing to seek some mental health help if I felt I needed it. Seeking help for my mental health issues saved my life several times over the span of my twenty-five-year career. At his point in my life, everything on the surface was picture perfect, but once again I had to get help.

As for the job at the Air Force Academy, we still had a good team. Our new commander was a young guy who I think they wanted to give a leadership opportunity. He was energetic and had a good attitude, but I think he was in leadership earlier than he should have been. When he came in, I thought back on the things that I could have helped my previous commander with, and I tried to help him. The ambition of this young commander was admirable, but it sometimes caused him to get ahead of himself and make mistakes. But we had just lost our previous commander, so there was no way this new commander would get fired—the air force would not let that happen to us twice in one year. So the colonel asked me to make sure the squadron did not fail. It was daunting to add that on top of everything else that had been building up over the last few years, but the commander and I got along well.

The Air Force Academy was a great experience. We had Division I sports, the largest being football, with exciting crowds of around forty thousand spectators for home games. I was in a coveted position in the air force on a college campus. Roughly eight months into my tenure, I felt like I was in one of the lowest physical and mental places of my life—even lower than seventeen years earlier at Maxwell, when I had contemplated taking my life. It wasn't the commanders or the work, per se. I just hadn't addressed the emotional baggage of so many things being added over the years, especially my most recent three years in England.

Air Force Academy football game

Mile 26 of the Bataan Death March

But this time I was older and more mature. I wasn't thinking about killing myself. It was just that it took me more time to roll out of bed in the morning and get moving. I was nearing twenty years in the air force. I had stayed in because I wanted to take care of my family, and I loved every minute of it. But I think parts of me had always been asking, *What do I want to do with my life? Do I want to be a teacher, author, or public speaker?* It wasn't about wanting to quit. I felt like I had given it my all, and it was time to take care of myself.

I was about four months away from putting on chief master sergeant. When you become a chief, you're required to sign a three-year service agreement. At this point, I was ready to step away from a long-term commitment to the air force. I decided I was going to call my career field manager, the top chief master sergeant for security forces. I'd ask for a waiver to get out of the air force early. I would turn down the stripe and retire as a senior master sergeant after twenty years of service, get my family back to a good place, and move on with my life.

The career field manager was actually the chief I had just worked with at space command HQ a year earlier. He told me to think about my decision a little more and to think about what I really needed right then. I had guilt from Lakenheath—from troops dying on my watch—and guilt over being an absent husband and father. After some reflection, I felt that what I really needed was to go downrange and get back into the front of things, where I could make the most impact. Although I wanted to retire, I felt I had unfinished business. I wanted to lead in a deployed environment again. I was being pressured to leave security forces for leadership positions, but I felt I still owed more to the countless airmen in my career field. At that moment in my career, getting bigger titles did not appeal to me. If I was going to stay, it had to be leading at the point of impact, which was the squadron. My commander at Lakenheath—the one who had to cut his Mediterranean cruise short in response to the terrorist incident—was down in the desert in the Middle East as a top colonel in force protection. We talked over the phone as well, and he said, "Absolutely not," to my idea of retiring. Did I want to go to Qatar and be a senior enlisted leader in charge of force protection for deployed troops?

Absolutely. I felt like it was the right thing to do. Although it would be a demanding job usually reserved for a more experienced chief master sergeant, it was the change I needed. I would be in charge of affecting base security for thousands of security forces, but I was up for the challenge. I needed something different.

I talked with my wife. She gave me the green light. My family was not in a great place at that time, and I thought this deployment might help us, as well. I accepted the role, but looking back on it, I'm not entirely sure I made the right decision from a family perspective, even with her blessing. My family stayed in Colorado Springs. In Qatar, I met one of the best leaders I've ever had, CZ. I was also in the senior enlisted leader for the headquarters staff and filled in as the command chief while he was out. I traveled 150 days out of the 365 days of that deployment. I visited troops in Jordan, Oman,

Afghanistan, Saudi Arabia, Kuwait, and other places. I flew back a few times to visit my family. I was at a point of impact, helping to shore up bases that had been attacked, helping them get the right equipment, weapons, and security systems. My work had purpose, and that year went by very fast.

Baptism site on the River Jordan

I'll never forget a conversation I had with CZ at the end of the year. I wasn't in a *Why not me?* mode, but more of a *Why me?* mode. I was excited to get back home to my family and wondering where I would go. I was competing for a MAJCOM job as functional manager at Wright

Patterson Air Force Base in Ohio, a top job in security forces. I once again felt like my career was on track and people were seeing me for my worth, and I was feeling mentally resilient.

CZ and I went into the dining facility, and over lunch he asked me what I wanted to do. I told him I was excited about the idea of holding another leadership position in security forces but that I was also thinking about leaving the air force. Then he asked me, "So, what do you think about being a command chief?" Incidentally, the wing commander at the Air Force Academy had suggested that, but I didn't feel like the time was right for my family or me. It would have been disingenuous to take an opportunity just because it was there, and I told CZ that. He asked, "Well, what about now?" My priority was to get back to my family. I gave him kind of a nonanswer. He was straight with me. "The General and I both believe you will be a great command chief."

Respectfully, I said if I was going to continue in the air force, I wanted to continue in security forces, where my passion had been reignited by my most recent Middle East tour. I told him that some of my ideas about leadership didn't match up with a command chief's responsibilities. Looking, back I had a one-sided view of the job. He said, "I believe you'll do this and do it well with your leadership style. The way you've been leading is how it should be done."

CZ is a leader among leaders. Although I had initially given him some pushback, I have great respect for him and how he carried himself. If he felt that my brand of leadership was the right fit for command chief,

I took it as a badge of honor and was all in. In a way, this conversation came at the right place and the right time. Just a year earlier, I had the same conversation with my wing command chief and wing commander. Even though I respected them as well, I still said no.

Three months later the command chief list came out. I didn't hear about it at PT this time. I was nominated to be a command chief. We had been living on the Wright Patterson Air Force Base in Ohio. Things were looking better for my family. We loved the Beaver Creek area. My oldest daughter had a full scholarship to the University of Alabama. My wife and I were reconnecting and going to shows, and our youngest daughter was already a freshman in high school. We had moved around pretty frequently in the last few years, and I hoped we were going to be in Ohio a few years to give our family more stability.

After the command chief list came out, another opportunity came up. My new MAJCOM command chief called and said I was on the short list to attend Air War College. This would be the first time they allowed chiefs to attend, and they were only selecting four. He said he needed to know if I was interested by the end of the day so he could tell the chief master sergeant of the air force. As soon as I got off the phone, I felt like I should go for it. But then I thought a little more about it. After committing to the air force, I had been running hard. I had taken every opportunity in front of me, but it had frequently come at the cost of uprooting my family out of one place and needing to replant ourselves in another. I knew that despite the opportunity, this would be a mistake in regard to some of the other things that really mattered to me. The other option was to go alone and leave my family behind, which would not have been good, either. I respectfully turned down the opportunity.

As it turned out, we would still be moving. When the list came out, I found out I was going to interview for the position at Edwards Air Force Base in California. I had never lived in California, but I'd always heard that base was in the middle of nowhere. I interviewed with a one-star general, and he told me I got the job only a few days later.

Ten months into Ohio, we moved to California. Even though I had initially wanted to leave the air force, my career in the air force was going well while my wife had become a civilian and a government service employee. She actually got promoted a day before my interview. But when I got the position at Edwards, she turned it down. It was heart-wrenching because I knew how much she wanted to progress in her own career, which was often on hold because we had to move around so much. On the drive to California, I was thinking, *Man, did I make the right decision? Here we go on our third move in just a few short years.* For those in the military, moving frequently can be tough on a family. We honor the sacrifices of our service members, but we forget the immense sacrifices their families make.

When we got to California, it also turned out to be great. Yes, Edwards was in the Mojave Desert, and it was a bit of a drive to get to different places off base, but we loved the area and made great friends. I learned so much from my new supervisor—the general who had interviewed me. He was an amazing leader. He was very inclusive in terms of diversity and in terms of learning. He was always willing to learn and grow from the people around him. Sometimes being in a job for several decades can make people think they know everything. But I was always learning from him.

Throwing out the first pitch in California

Most of what I was doing now involved the bigger picture of how the entire air force operated, not just how one base operated. It broadened my perspective. That opportunity at Edwards changed my entire career and how

I looked at the air force. Prior to Edwards, I looked at things in my immediate circumstances. At Edwards—the largest test wing in USAF, where every new aircraft was tested—I saw the latest cutting-edge technology before it was released, and I even flew on some of those aircrafts. I was seeing the bigger picture.

Today, this general is a three-star general, but back then, he was about to get his second star. He asked if I would go with him to his next assignment to keep the team together. I was thrilled. I was coming up on a year of working with him, and his request made me want to stay in the air force. Additionally, staying could have meant we would remain at Edwards, which would have given us some long-term stability. One day I got a text from my MAJCOM chief while I was visiting a strategic school in El Paso, Texas:

Would you be interested in being the command chief at Air University?

As I looked at this text on the phone, I was stunned. Would I become the command chief of Air University? I was taken aback. Maxwell was my first base. It was where I had thought about taking my own life, and it was where I experienced some of the most overt racism I had ever experienced, which threw me into that funk in the first place. I never ever envisioned myself ever returning there. I had been in the air force for twenty-two years already.

I remember sitting on my bed, contemplating it all. *What do I do in this situation?* Accepting a position recommended by the chief master sergeant of the air force and the MAJCOM command chief? They wanted me to lead education for the entire United States Air Force. I thought to myself, *These people don't know my story—failing fourth and ninth grade, barely graduating high school, barely getting into the air force, going through my depression.*

They knew college professor Todd Simmons, public-speaking Todd Simmons, blogging Todd Simmons. They didn't know the Todd Simmons who could barely read and barely made it through math—the one who made bad life choices. I really was having a self-confidence check. *Can I do this?* Even though I had five college degrees, was a college professor, had written curricula, and streamlined development, I still had a self-confidence dilemma inside, regardless of my résumé. On the outside was a confident leader with a callous mindset. On the inside, I was struggling.

But then I got up off the bed where I had been thinking it over. I just felt like the biggest thing for me was returning to Maxwell—the scene of the crime, so to speak. At that moment, something dawned on me. It was bigger than the question of *Why not me?* that had constantly followed me. It was this inner knowing that I absolutely had to take this position at Maxwell—that I had unfinished business there. I said to myself, *That year you spent there, twenty-one years ago, almost cost you your life. You have something to prove, and you've got to go back there and finish that business.* I remember those thoughts going through my head.

That's when it settled in—the question of *Why not me?* from a different angle. *Why not me* for this job? Who cares if I had these issues in my past? I turned them around. *Why not me?*

So I decided I *would* like to interview for the position; I was excited for this opportunity. I interviewed twice.

The first interview was with the general who was leaving the position. I didn't hear anything back. When those kinds of situations play out, it's always easy to think, *I didn't get the job.* But then I got another call to interview again—this time with the incoming general who would be my supervisor. A little while later, I was at Starbucks on Edwards Air Force Base. The phone call came as I was in the middle of my order. The incoming general was on the phone asking me how I'd like to join the team.

I got an overwhelming feeling of joy and validation.

Everything comes when it comes for a reason. Everything happens in this life for a reason. I knew that I was going to Air University for a reason. It was just too clear to me because of what had happened to me there two decades ago. So I told my boss, and he was happy for me. Our family prepared to go to Alabama. There were certain parts that would just work out for our family; our daughter was already going to school an hour away. But then, some anxiety started to kick in. So much of it was about going back to Maxwell.

12

The best revenge is massive success.
—Frank Sinatra

MAXWELL WAS WHERE SO MUCH life-changing stuff had happened, but I hadn't told my wife about any of it yet. As we left Edwards, I felt a little guilty about how our constant moving affected my wife's career. She had difficulty securing a job when we were at Edwards, and when she finally got one, we moved again seven months later. Just a decade earlier she was on her way to a solid career in the air force, and that had flipped on over to me. Knowing that drove me to reach for success. If I was the one staying in the service, I would have to succeed at what I was doing.

So we drove from California to Alabama. We made some stops along the way; my wife had always wanted to see the Grand Canyon. I cannot say I was such a great travel partner. I had this nervous energy during the whole trip; I just had so much anxiety. I was headed into this huge responsibility for leading and developing education across the entire air force. I felt like a spotlight was going to shine on me and that I couldn't fail. I was worried about getting found out. What if they learned about my past? Looking back, I realized I should have asked myself, *What was I going to be "found out" about?* I had two MA degrees. I had been to the FBI National Academy. I had accolades from our operations in Korea. But behind all that, I saw myself as a kid from Hardeeville who barely got into the air force and who barely passed college algebra. It was thoughts like this that kept me quiet on the entire trip.

We arrived at Maxwell. As we drove through the gates and checked in, I still had so much anxiety. There was no real fanfare around our arrival. It wasn't what I was used to in the past, but I was happy we got to slip in almost unnoticed. There were some gift baskets in our room, but no one met us in person other than the executive NCO who would be my assistant. I think I was actually happy about the reception being low-key because I was nervous about this totally new type of job. I had been used to leading people on the ground, and this would be a more administrative, big-picture kind of role. The stakes seemed higher, as I was going from working with a one-star general to working with a three-star general.

We started setting up our life in Montgomery, which included enrolling my youngest daughter in high school. As it turned out, the school system there was not that great, and the high school she would be going to was low rated. They did have charter schools in the area, but that wasn't an option for us because we missed the enrollment deadline. So we made a decision to put her in a private school. We didn't come into the military to get rich, especially since we came through on the enlisted side, so this was a serious financial decision. My older daughter had a full scholarship to the University of Alabama. My younger daughter had a 4.0, and I didn't want to risk her losing that to a challenging environment.

The general and I made it a priority to ensure that military kids and even civilian kids there were getting an education from a system that took its responsibility seriously. We worked with state and city governments and secured provisions for military families moving to low-income areas to enroll in charter schools so they wouldn't have to choose between paying for private school or sending their kids to a poor performing public school. I'm not against public school. My kids went to public schools in Colorado and California, but the school system in Montgomery was not good. My daughter came from a good academic background, so we were willing to pay $14,000 per year for two years for her to receive a better education.

So, I was already starting off in Maxwell facing this significant financial commitment. It's one I wanted to take, but it was coming in on top of my bad memories of the place. And yet, I would do it all over again. I knew my background and what my experience was like going through a school system that was too resource poor to care about the students. That's why I raised my kids to place academic excellence over everything, because that's something nobody can ever take away.

A command chief lives on base, traditionally in a home designated for that purpose. But they didn't have that kind of setup at Maxwell, so they just designated an available home for us. These were historic homes, roughly eighty-six years old. I remember when I was at Maxwell, I'd drive around these beautiful 4,000-square-foot homes, where the colonels and generals lived. Come Christmastime, they'd be decked out with their lights, and I would think about who lived in those stately mansions.

Here I was, the highest-ranking enlisted person on the base, and I was one of the few enlisted personnel to live in one of these homes. As we were moving, I went over to the house to meet the movers, who had parked their truck in the front of the property. I had entered the house from the back and walked out the front door to meet them. I didn't know what I was about to see as I walked out the front door.

The house was elevated above the street by a set of stairs, which allowed me to look over the airfield. My eyes fixated on the exact spot where over twenty-one years earlier I had been talking on the phone to my mom, telling her I wanted to kill myself. It was an emotional moment for me, seeing that spot and reflecting on where I had come since then. Remember, this house was not a designated house for a command chief—they just assigned us a random available house. But the fact that this house had a view of that exact spot made me know I was brought back to Maxwell for a reason. I had one of the strongest convictions I've ever had about this turn of events. As I was looking at that spot, I felt like someone had put a VHS tape into my mind and pushed fast-forward, and my whole life went in front of my eyes for a minute or so. Once the business of the move settled down, I shared that moment with my wife.

Air University Command Chief residence

Public speaking would play a major part in my responsibilities at Air University. Although I am a public speaker today, when I was selected as the command chief for Air University, I was absolutely not a public speaker. I was good in a class of thirty to forty people as a college professor or training law enforcement personnel, but I was not a true public speaker. When I traveled around the bases in the Middle East to shore up security, I would talk to larger crowds, maybe one hundred strong, about equipment I needed to get them. But this would be totally different, and one of the biggest responsibiiities my new role entailed was public speaking.

The general I was working for when I first came to Maxwell would be moving on in about four months, so

I went into the role as the team was in transition. For the first three months, I was just trying to learn what the organization was doing. I didn't build a real bond with that general. What I later learned is that the exiting general didn't want to hire me. But the incoming general wanted me there out of all the candidates.

Over the next three or four months, I was getting the hang of the job. Then one day, I got a call from the commandant at the Senior NCO Academy, a prestigious institution for enlisted professional education. He asked if I would be the guest speaker at their commencement. There were 400 students graduating, not to mention family in the room. I had never been a speaker for anything of this magnitude. I was terrified, but I said absolutely.

I had to make a decision: Was I going to write a speech, or not write one and just speak on the spot? I decided to go with writing a speech. I looked at it for two weeks, over and over again. The big day came. I put on my service dress, and I went to speak.

There was a restroom for instructors right by the auditorium. I stepped in to have a few moments of privacy, and then I started throwing up in the stall. I had some ginger ale and water with me, and I was freaking out. I remember thinking to myself, *Here I am, in one of the biggest jobs I will ever have. And in five minutes, I have to go out into a room with hundreds of people who are going to be looking at me, and I'm going to have to say something.*

Somehow I got myself together in front of the mirror. Later, I read a book by a Navy SEAL, David Goggins, *Can't Hurt Me*, which gave me the idea of an accountability mirror. I made my own routine out of it, and I've been doing this every day since. Every morning I took time to reflect in the mirror. Sometimes it was silent, and sometimes it was verbal. It was born out of controlling my anxiety and getting my day set up with confidence. One of my favorite mantras became "being comfortable; being uncomfortable." In other words, get comfortable with challenging situations. For example, I was pretty uncomfortable with public speaking, so I went out and found every public speaking engagement I could find that year. I trained myself to get comfortable with it.

At that moment, in the restroom outside the auditorium, that mirror routine came in real handy. I gripped that sink, looked in the mirror, and said, "You got this." I came out of the restroom and confronted my two options. I was going to deliver the speech at the podium in a more natural position. I hate speaking behind a podium. I'm more natural standing by myself. Meanwhile, my speech was crinkled up because I had been gripping it over and over again while I practiced the previous two weeks. But what I was going to talk about was already in my mind.

In the end, I chose not to go to the podium. I didn't even go up on the stage. I stood where I could see the whole crowd and delivered a seventeen-minute speech. At that moment, I knew I could do this public speaking thing. I said to myself, *Why not me? Why have I been running away from any opportunity to speak my story and inspire people who needed to hear it?* I think the prestige of the school spooked me, as well. But I had to rebuild my confidence over and over again and grow out of my comfort zone. I made the speech, and that was that. I got a lot of positive feedback on that speech because I shared about leadership in a relatable way without reading from note cards about the topic. It was real talk from my heart.

The incoming general and I were a great team. We built a relationship on trust and connection. At this point, I was in a high-profile position. My wife was never a fan of the social aspects of the command chief world, but the general was very accommodating about that. A command chief's wife is expected to show up at events or host her own. My wife was a great NCO and officer in her own right, and now she was a government service worker. She was independent, and playing a socialite role did not fit her personality. So we made a deal: If she wanted to come with me to events or not, that was fine. She could make pursuing her own career a priority. The incoming general and his wife were an awesome team, great family friends, and they accommodated our family goals. They made us feel comfortable and didn't hold us to social expectations. They even felt like older siblings to us. We would go to their house for dinner and do other stuff together. We were fortunate to be teamed up with them.

Now that the incoming general had entered the scene, our task really began. I was charged with redefining enlisted education. We revamped multiple courses. I was speaking around seven times and traveling ten days out of every month. Revamping education for the 300,000 airmen in the air force was a huge task. Over the next year, I went from never speaking publicly to doing around 100 engagements per year.

One day I got a call from Junior ROTC, which was

in charge of around 800 Junior ROTC detachments in high schools and 147 ROTC detachments at universities. They wanted me to come to their worldwide master drill competition in Daytona Beach, Florida, and be the guest speaker at the awards ceremony. This was a massive event. My confidence was built at this point, but this was an opportunity to really level up my confidence. I headed down to Daytona.

The awards ceremony was in a soccer stadium. I walked in to see around five thousand people there and a speaker's podium in the middle of the field. It was a real *wow* moment. I had my speech in a binder. I stepped up to the podium, opened the binder, looked around at the crowd, and then I closed it. I took the mic and started walking through the crowd as I spoke from my heart. That moment was transformative. I thought to myself, *I can truly do this*. Seventy-five speeches after throwing up in the bathroom at my first major speaking engagement, I was speaking to thousands of people in a stadium setting.

I gave hundreds of speeches over the next two years as part of my job. I rarely used notes. My speeches were personal and came from my own experiences, observations, and feelings. I didn't want to speak strategically or in a planned, measured way. I wanted to connect with the audience.

Meanwhile, we were transforming the curriculum in air force education. I was on the board of the community college for the air force, as well. The air force was the only service that offered airmen its own community college, and I helped set up a task force to revamp the program for the first time in two decades. I was sitting on multiple boards and task forces for policy and development in promotion and education for officers and enlisted personnel. The general put me in charge of marketing Air University as well. One of my jobs was to go around to different bases and speak about the university.

I started a video series called *That's Air University*. They were one-minute videos of people who came to the organization from around the air force. We had a great videographer and team who were able to get the message together in one-minute clips that were hard-hitting. I filmed a bunch of people I knew to be in the clips who would be natural advocates and influencers. I really felt in my element doing all this curriculum development and promotional speaking. This was the height of my career. Education and development were things I had become very familiar with, and I was doing what I loved.

It was hard to believe that at one point, I hadn't read a book cover to cover, and now I was in charge of education for the entire air force. It had to be everything I wanted. I wasn't in the air force to chase something like promotion or titles. I was just happy to serve today and see what tomorrow brings. As it was, I had already tried to get out of the air force and turn down a chief stripe. I just loved the job. I still had the desire more than ever to be a teacher. Some people reminded me that one day I could be a chief master sergeant of the air force. Every time I heard that, it would not resonate; it's not that I wasn't appreciative of their belief in me. It was just that I wasn't serving for titles. I wanted to be purposeful.

My wife and I had been talking about the possibility of me retiring for about six years. It wasn't because I didn't like what I was doing. Honestly, there was nothing else that I could have done in the air force that would have been better for me than what I was doing at Air University.

It took about a year on the job at Maxwell before I set foot in the security forces squadron building where I heard that racist conversation and plotting so many years ago. I only drove over to that building because I had been invited to speak. Nobody around me knew it, but I had the highest degree of anxiety going in there. So many memories started coming back to me. I was blown away that it was pretty much exactly the same building on the inside. It was like I walked in, and it was 1995 again. I was talking to the chief of the squadron and a few others with us, telling them little facts about the building, saying things like, "This room used to be the weight room." I had this nervous energy about me, giving a historical tour of their building, but they couldn't see that.

We walked around the corner, and I faced the spot where that mirror was, where so many years ago I had been adjusting my uniform and overheard that conversation. But now the mirror was gone. I told them all about the mirror—how airmen would stand there and get ready for their shift. The commander was excited about the idea, saying he would love to put that mirror back up. I wanted to say, "No, don't do that," but obviously I didn't say anything about it. It's not that the mirror itself was bad, but the memory was just too overpoweringly bad for me to embrace that idea. The break room was still a break room, with the same two soda machines and a snack machine. I talked to their troops, but after that event, I only went there one other time when I had to promote someone. The building always gave me an uneasy feeling.

While all this exciting work was going on with the public speaking and making the promotional videos, I took another positive turn with mental health. I didn't really have an option other than to seek help. Everything I had experienced and shouldered at Lakenheath—and even Maxwell the first time around—was coming back to me. There was also a recent family tragedy that I hadn't processed, which occurred shortly after I arrived at Maxwell.

One year after I arrived at Air University, the older of my two sisters was having a serious cancer relapse. My sister and her husband visited me in England and other places we were stationed. They took care of our kids during deployments. They were fairly involved in my life. Growing up, my older sister had given a helpful hand in raising me while our mom worked two or three jobs. My older sister and I became closer, as we were the only two left in the house after my older brother left, and my second sister moved out. Our relationship improved significantly once she started dating her future husband, Jonathan. I spent a lot of time with them while my mom worked multiple jobs. She married when I was ten, but her husband had been like a brother to me. He would pick me up and take me around bargain hunting, and I think he kept me out of trouble. He taught me how to shop for deals in the clearance section or at the pawn shop. He was a male figure who shaped how I thought about certain things. Later in life, I learned a lot from him about family values and how to raise children by watching him raise my nieces. He always bought them nice clothes and made sure they had what they needed.

My sister developed cancer, had surgery, and had gone into remission. The cancer had come back. In November, we went home for Thanksgiving, where I saw my sister. She was frail and had low energy. I was worried, but I had seen her go back and forth through this disease. We returned to Maxwell, and her husband would call with updates, often telling me she was getting worse.

One day, I got a call as my wife and I were leaving the theater. I could tell what was going on right away. My brother-in-law was a strong person, so his voice gave it away. My sister was sick again. I responded that I was going to come home soon. I knew I was going to see her in February and thought it was just part of the cycle and that she would get better. Then, he called me at work shortly after that. She was sick. I said, "Okay—I'll be there next week."

I'll always remember the words he said after that: "Next week will be too late." He wasn't sure she would last another day or two.

He got a little loud with me because I was asking questions to resist what he was telling me. I don't think I ever let myself believe she was that sick. "You need to get here," he told me. I went to my executive NCO. I couldn't think straight. I called my wife and told her what was going on. I drove home and grabbed things that didn't even match out of my drawers because I had no time to pack. It all went down in fifteen minutes. I got on the highway in my uniform. My niece, who had also been in the air force but was separated with an active-duty husband, was driving in from Texas at the same time. I remember us talking. I could not process what was going on.

I arrived at my sister's house, and I walked in to find my mom, my other sister, everyone. My brother-in-law came out of a back room, where my sister was in a hospital bed. He told me to prepare myself. I walked in, and I wasn't prepared. My sister was on life support and could barely breathe. Her two daughters were in there comforting her. I broke down so hard that my legs gave way. I got carried out and needed to get myself together before going back into her. I had to process this all and tell her goodbye. She was not speaking anymore, but I told her I loved her. That was our last moment together. At that moment, I realized all the family baggage I never faced. I ran to the military and never addressed anything from my childhood. I just felt there was always time, but that moment gave me another pivotal life lesson: face your demons head-on.

After that I went to my mom's house. Within three hours, my brother-in-law called and said my sister had passed away. It was the biggest loss I had experienced in my life. I never had any other loss feel so deep, so gut-wrenching, and so wounding. My sister's death had affected me in a way that no other death had. But I tucked it away when I went back to work.

I think that's what contributed to a general feeling of anxiety I started to develop. This was something new. I had felt anxiety before, but now I was having what almost felt like anxiety attacks over nothing. It was overwhelming to me. I decided to speak to the chaplain and then a military and family life counselor (MFLC) who was a civilian social worker who met with military personnel. It could be helpful to meet with an MFLC because service members might be reluctant to share what's bothering them with someone else in the military. Although there might be less of it today, there has been a stigma that has prevented service members from seeking mental health treatment.

Unfortunately, the air force had seen a rise in suicides over the years. I used to get the monthly suicide stats and write-ups about young people killing themselves. I've had a few people share their story with me, as well, and I knew people were struggling. But it also seemed like people were ashamed to check in with other people about their mental health journey. It wasn't that I hadn't already realized this, but it just really dawned on me one day in particular as I was sitting in my office. I have always suffered through problems and challenges, both in my personal life and throughout my military career. I thought to myself, *Where has there been a safe space for me to talk about this kind of stuff?* I couldn't think of many.

My executive assistant and I were preparing to travel and give a presentation on Air University. At this particular event, there were about four hundred to five hundred people in the auditorium. I used to start these presentations with a video from the general, who was all about empowering the enlisted force. Although he himself was an officer, the general's father was a retired chief master sergeant, so he had grown up in the military and was familiar with its enlisted side and its values.

But that day just playing the presentation didn't feel right. I looked out over the crowd and turned the presentation off. I just started talking about resilience and my own personal journey as I walked off the stage and into the crowd. I had all the stripes the air force could give—and a command chief star to boot—but I don't think anyone in that crowd had ever heard someone with that rank talking about this kind of stuff from a place of personal experience. I could feel people opening up.

I essentially did a presentation on what resilience looks like in the air force, what it looks like in our families, and what it looks like in our own personal struggles. I shared that I've struggled, but I've also been successful. And if I could put one thing on my success, it would be that at my lowest point I had someone to hold on to. Lakenheath could have cost me my marriage and my life because I was depressed. Maxwell could have cost me my life. I emphasized the importance of seeking help.

We packed our stuff up after the presentation and walked out. I thought to myself, *What did I just do?* I didn't know if I had done the right thing or how this would be received. I was worried the leadership would not ask me to come back. I had talked about this kind of stuff a little bit in small groups, but I had never done that in a public forum of that size.

People were waiting for me at the door. I was shaking hands with people who were saying things like, "Thank you for being transparent. We never had a leader talk like this." I was a little scared of the feedback, honestly. But it continued to come in. I got emails and messages thanking me for that talk.

Our team continued traveling. The next event we went to was a big conference where I would be speaking to two large groups. It was at this point I decided to formalize my resiliency talk. I created a presentation called *How Much*

Are You Carrying? It's a question I asked throughout the presentation, and the answer involved going through my own life. I got everyone in the audience to look through theirs, and it ended with a sixty-day challenge to look in a mirror every day for some time. I told them about looking themselves in the mirror and being accountable to themselves. I also told everyone to reconcile with people from their pasts—to at least get what they needed to get off their chests. I talked about how I went back to my own family and reconciled to the best of my ability. I discussed creating a plan to move forward.

When I first delivered the formalized presentation to around seven hundred people, everyone started walking out, and I thought, *Am I offending people here?* But they were walking out because they were crying. This talk was bringing up things they were dealing with that maybe they hadn't confronted. The same thing happened in the second group. I had a line of people about thirty deep waiting to talk to me after the presentation. People have asked me how I can stand in a room and talk about the deepest parts of my life. During this conference, I was emotionally spent. I talked with so many people, heard so many stories, and really saw the true measure of the pain people were carrying around in secret.

I gave about forty more of those presentations. What these talks did for me personally was that they showed me something important: not only does everyone have a story, but in a position of leadership, that story can be a script for people who believe their story won't get better. Although it was rewarding, that presentation took a lot out of me. Anytime I gave that presentation, I had to take a two-hour nap afterward. No matter how many times I relived the shame of failing in school or not feeling wanted by my dad, it was still very difficult bringing those things up. It brought up new ways of looking at those things I hadn't suffered through already. It was hard, but it helped other people.

My self-reflection and this entire process of creating that presentation also helped me with my own health. We had to get physical health assessments every year in the air force. Part of that assessment involved filling out a form and answering how we felt physically and mentally from one to ten. The questionnaire asked us about suicide. I will be honest: We routinely filled them out incorrectly because we didn't want any hassle or shame coming our way. Many didn't want to jeopardize their careers.

When the day came for me to fill out this form, I filled it out like I always did, and then I erased the perfunctory marks I had put down. I decided I was going to think through these questions and answer them honestly. As a command chief, I was in a very public spotlight. My picture was up on many places around the base, practically in every building. When I handed my form over, the tech looked down at it and probably thought it was going to be routine. And there I was, thinking about making big decisions regarding my career. I was tired of traveling. I was stressed out. My daughter was going through her own challenges from the frequent moves over the years. I wanted to help her, but I couldn't. She ended up going through her own mental health journey. There was a lot going on, and I put it all down on the form.

The tech was caught off guard and took my form back

somewhere. What I didn't know was that once the form was filled out, I would be scheduled to talk to someone. So, I went and talked to this individual. She looked at my rank, then my answers, and then a chart on her board with air force ranks on it. She said she had never seen someone of my rank in fourteen years of doing this work. I didn't take that as a positive at all. Honestly, I felt ashamed. We're not immune to problems. I knew a chief master sergeant, E9, who killed himself in his office. That permanently affected me because I had talked to him over Facebook Messenger twenty-four hours before he killed himself. I didn't know what was going on with him, but it was a serious example that senior-ranking airmen were not immune to mental health issues.

It ended up being a phenomenal session. I felt comfortable talking to her. I even went back for more help. On that particular day, after I left the session, I turned my phone on and filmed a video of myself—a candid video about getting help. Getting help needed to be proactive and preventative, not reactive. I talked about the importance of filling out that form correctly and the shame around mental health issues that led people to not being honest in their answers.

I was a public figure as a senior leader, but I still posted that video on social media. It got tens of thousands of views, and I received hundreds of direct messages. It stimulated a conversation and made people think of their own situations. Posting that video came out of the character I had developed over the previous two years. I was willing to be uncomfortable if I could help someone else realize it was okay to get help. I was willing to do things like that if I could be a source of inspiration. It became a mantra: being comfortable; being uncomfortable.

Every day I would drive past the spot where I wanted to kill myself to one of the biggest houses on the base. Then I was a young kid. Now I was married with two kids of my own. I incorporated my mental health journey into my presentations. At that point, I had hundreds of speaking engagements under my belt. I had traveled all over. My wife and I were discussing my retirement. The chief master sergeant of the air force was an advocate and a friend, and he asked me if I wanted to compete for a MAJCOM command chief position in Europe. I talked to my wife. My wife always wanted what was best for me.

I never wanted to let anyone down. But at the same time, I was torn. I felt like I had more to give if the opportunity presented itself. But at the same time, if presented with the opportunity to retire, I could choose that path. I felt like I had more to give outside the air force. This crossroads felt like a win-win. Either I would go to Europe to be the MAJCOM command chief, or we'd live our dream of by making society better outside the air force.

I got interviewed by a general in Europe. We talked for about forty minutes. This interview had actually been postponed two times already. I feel that I was a great communicator, and I can really feel out a conversation, especially from some of the training I took at the FBI National Academy, where I learned techniques on reading folks during interviews and interrogations. The first ninety seconds gave me everything I needed to know. I do not believe we made a connection during the conversation, which led me to believe one of two things: I wasn't the guy he wanted to hire, or I was just reading into it too much, and the sterility of our exchange was more of a personality issue I would have to navigate. By contrast, when I had interviewed for the positions at Edwards and Air University, the discussion was extremely personal and even family oriented. This one did not feel that way.

People were rooting for me to get that job. I spoke to my current boss. I said I didn't think I got the job; I didn't think we gelled on the phone.

A week passed by, and I was told the general who had interviewed me wanted to call me. I knew the results. He called to give me the news that he decided to go in another direction. I sincerely thanked him for the opportunity.

But we had made up our minds. It was now or never to make the decision to retire. That would not have been the only job for me. There were other opportunities coming fast. My wife and I spoke about it, and I said, "I think at this point I have rolled the dice on the craps table and won millions. It's time to take my winnings and walk away." Looking back on it all, I had barely gotten into the air force in the first place. That recruiter could have said no and walked away. At one point, early on in my career, I had tried to kill myself. I could barely read. I couldn't write. Through it all, I made rank. I got promoted fast. I went to the FBI National Academy. I became one of three hostage negotiators in the USAF. I obtained two MAs. I got married and had kids. Most importantly, I recognized I needed help before it was too late, and I was now in a good place mentally and physically.

We looked at the pros and cons of retiring. There seemed to be nothing but pros, actually. My wife's career could get back on track. She had spent ten years in the same grade of government service because we kept moving around. Every time she got a promotion, we had to move. She was—and is—an intelligent, talented woman who deserved to succeed professionally.

I decided it was time for me to cash in my winnings. It was time to take what I got and go out and continue to do good for people—still for people in the military but also now for the community. I would be coming out of the military with talents, access to better resources, and education. I could use that to help people.

The next day I walked into my general's office and announced I would be retiring. He was surprised. He wanted me to stick around. I said, "Sir, I've stuck around in the air force. I'm forty-three. I have the ambition to do two things beyond the USAF. I want to improve education in underserved communities, and I want to run for political office." I truly believe, and I have believed this ever since the eighth grade, that education is the gateway to a better future.

I explained that all to the chief master sergeant of the air force, and he understood. "But if you want to stick around . . ." he added.

I replied, "It's not that I don't want to stay, or that I don't like what I'm doing. It's about passion and desire. I want to take what the air force gave me and share it with the outside world."

My retirement ceremony was scheduled for December

6, 2019, around nine months after I told the general my decision to retire. I had never been more excited about the next chapter of my life. It's interesting—just as spontaneously as my wife and I had gotten married, we were going to exit the air force. The only reason I wanted the ceremony was because I wanted to create an environment with a family emphasis. The person who retired me was my first cousin, my mom's nephew, who had also joined the air force and today is a one-star general. We shared the bond of being two very successful Black men in the military. My oldest daughter sang the national anthem. I had a good friend act as master of ceremonies—a friend who later became the nineteenth chief master sergeant of the air force and the first female senior enlisted leader of any service. The whole event had a family flair. I didn't care about how many people attended, but I cared that my family would be sharing this moment. We left a seat open for my sister who had passed away.

My mom, surviving sister, and brother were all there. This was the first time in twenty-five years that my family had been to a military event. But that did not bother me. If they were going to attend anything, it should've been that day. I had friends from all over the world show up. Someone who had worked for me flew all the way in from Japan to Alabama just to come to the retirement ceremony. One of my best friends came, who happened to be the staff sergeant I had worked with in Alaska. He was retired already. The chief master sergeant of the air force showed up and gave my wife a certificate.

I didn't want the ceremony to be about me, actually, and I waved off all the formalities. I didn't get anything presented to me except the retirement medal. In fact, I talked about my wife's service. When my wife got out of the military, there was no fanfare or ceremony. She had put on her uniform one day and separated the next. It was like she didn't exist. She had carried some hard feelings about what happened to her in Iraq and after coming back. So I had secretly packed away all her shoulder boards and stripes and awards, setting them aside for something like that day. Traditionally, when airmen retired from the air force, they received a shadow box with all their stuff in it, like their rank or any medals they had earned. I had one made for me, but I didn't have it presented at the ceremony. What I did instead was cover up a custom-made shadow box for my wife, with everything that she had ever been awarded.

During my retirement speech, I talked about my wife's service, highlighting what many people there didn't know. She was an enlisted NCO, an officer, an Iraqi War veteran, an accomplished person, and someone who never got her own day. I had decided this was going to be her day. I presented her with that shadow box in front of everybody. I never saw her so emotional—I think it was everything she had held in all these years and not having any closure. If there was one last thing in the air force that I was going to do with my own stripes, stars, and power, it was honoring my wife, and that's the way I wanted to leave the United States Air Force.

Retirement Day, December 6, 2019

Coming full circle from a kid from a small town in South Carolina to traveling the world, I left the air force on top. I did everything I could to represent all those that looked up for inspiration. After my retirement, we moved to the Washington, DC area, where my wife's civilian career took off, and I started speaking professionally. Sixty days after we arrived in DC, we received a phone call. "Hello, I am from the Mayor's office." It was the mayor from the town of Hardeeville, South Carolina, where I grew up. They wanted to invite me back home for a special proclamation declaring February 6 CMSgt Todd Simmons

Day. Just think—the town of Hardeeville was honoring me. *Why Not Me!*

Speaking on resiliency in Kansas

MY NEXT CHAPTER —AND YOURS

My next stop is going to be all about helping people achieve their dreams. I don't want people to ask *Why not me?* from a place of negativity and thinking about what they don't have. I want people to ask that question from a place of empowerment and recognize what they can get. I want them to see and know—it is me. My dream is going into underserved communities and teaching people how to own opportunity, and how to believe. If you believe, you can overcome so much more.

All my challenges—with race, education, mental health, and family—just set me up to win. Are challenges difficult? Yes. Are there going to be barriers in life? Yes. But the most important question I want everyone who reads this book to walk away with is its title: *Why not me?*

Here are a few other reflections I want to leave with readers:

REFLECTION 1

GET OUTSIDE YOUR OWN BOX

I've also learned the importance of travel from the napkin that changed my life. Get out, see the world, and open your mind. You don't have to read an encyclopedia. Information is all over. Whatever you dream, you can achieve—and you don't have to be stuck anywhere. You can live in any state or visit any place, even if you aren't in the military. Go on Groupon and find a travel deal. Save money for two years. Get your eighty-nine-dollar passport and go to Greece, Paris, wherever. Visit a foreign country every few years—it's really more affordable than you think.

The best education I received was not earning five degrees; it was visiting forty-seven countries. Living in these different places and experiencing new worlds with all five senses was worth more than any college degree or class. Living in Japan and Korea changed my whole perspective. Same thing with the Middle East—to sit down and eat on the floor with bread instead of a fork. Having conversations with people of different perspectives is growth.

And you know what? You can even do this right here in the United States, wherever you live. Go to ethnic communities you aren't from and eat. I went to an Ethiopian restaurant recently. I talked to the waitress about where the spices were from, and I learned about Ethiopia—what a cultural melting pot it is and its history. I had been all over the world, and I didn't know that. You can always learn new things if you have an open mind and the right attitude about growth.

REFLECTION 2
YOU HAVE NO CEILING

FOR MUCH OF MY LIFE, I thought it could never be me. For anybody reading this book, I want them to know that it *can* be you. It's okay to wake up, look around, and see a world that isn't the way you want your reality to be. It's okay because that doesn't have to stay your reality. I woke up many days thinking I was less than and that my environment had a ceiling. I've learned since then that whatever you can dream, you can achieve, but it will take work. You will get a lot of doors closed in your face. There will be adversity. There will be tears. There will be people who don't believe you or who don't believe in you.

But it is possible to achieve what you dream—whatever that dream is for you. Maybe you see people who are wealthy or successful, and you wonder if you can get there. You can get educated about business and get yourself there. Maybe you see someone who has something intangible that you'd like to achieve, like a college degree or inner peace or whatever. You can also learn about how they got there and put in the work. But whatever it is that you aspire to, the overall goal is to get unstuck—to stop believing that your environment has a ceiling keeping you trapped, because the truth is that you can rise and continue to rise.

I think it's good to take the question of *Why not me?* to heart and be vocal about it. In my late twenties, I learned that you have to force people to see you. You can't sit back and say to yourself, *I'm doing a good job. Why am I not getting the attention I deserve? Why am I not getting the attention*

I need to get ahead in the game? I've learned the importance of communicating what you want so you can get what you deserve.

If I think I can't accomplish something, it actually fuels my desire to get it. I've known fear, shame, failure, and disappointment, but I've also learned that once you take them, own them, and use them as fuel—man, you can get past anything in your way. As for shame, I don't really have it anymore. If I screw something up, I'm okay with talking about it. I've already shared my deepest, darkest secrets. If I know I can't do something, I teach myself how to do it. For example, in recent years, I've taught myself how to wire. I make electrical stuff and give it away to friends. If something is difficult, I want to sit down and figure it out.

Education is the gateway to the future. Reading and self-improvement is free. You can go to the library or look up whatever you need to know on the internet. Surround yourself with people who have made it to where you want to be. Even if you can only find one person, get a mentor who may have faced the same challenges you faced or are facing, who can say, "Hey, here's what you need to do." Sometimes you will have to seek this mentorship out. Go to a small business owner and ask how they built their business. Find a veteran who has traveled the world. Find people you can surround yourself with who can change your perspective—people who can help you realize there is no ceiling.

REFLECTION 3
BE WILLING TO BE VULNERABLE

I WANT TO BE AN advocate for mental health. We cannot be afraid of mental health, and we've got to teach people it's okay to share their thoughts and emotions. We've got to see mental health the same as we see other types of health. All of us, every single human being, will go through something and not handle it well—whether they're a teenager crying over a crush or a forty-year-old crying over a totaled car. Life will deal you roadblocks. Sometimes you roll snake eyes. Sometimes you crap out. But you've got to reach out to someone when you need help.

It took me a long time to learn the power of vulnerability. I grew up not expressing feelings or embracing emotional connection with other people because showing emotion, especially something like crying, was a sign of weakness where I came from. But over time, I learned it's okay to take a step back and be vulnerable. In fact, I would tell you to use vulnerability as a superpower.

Vulnerability is not just about emotions; it's also about being brave enough to say out loud that you don't know something or that you need help. It took me a while to admit that I wouldn't understand math if I didn't show my vulnerable side. It took work to admit that I needed help in my marriage because I wasn't used to connecting with someone emotionally, or that I needed help in my job because I was overwhelmed.

Vulnerability is not a weakness. It's a strength that allows you to release those pressures building up inside of you and to shout out that you need help. And that's the most powerful thing you can do for yourself—to say, "I need help." But you have to take a step back and be vulnerable enough and not just say you need it but to receive it. Once you do, things will change. Things will turn around. But it all starts with being vulnerable, forgetting what people think about you, and embracing the honesty of asking for help because you want to be better—whether it's help with your mental health, work, or your relationships. You need to be vulnerable to know when you're stuck. And that's the simple superpower you have.

REFLECTION 4

ANYTHING IS POSSIBLE

Whether you're nineteen, twenty-nine, thirty-nine, or seventy-nine, reflection is a powerful thing. You can look back on times when you didn't think something was possible, and now you can say, "Wow, anything is possible." As I reflect on my own life, I'm amazed by some of the things that happened. I didn't think it would be possible for me to leave Hardeeville, be successful in the military, have people to listen to what I have to say, become a college professor, lead education for the entire United States Air Force, or put my story down in writing. But all that stuff has happened.

We all have things in our minds that we think are impossible. Don't let them defeat you. Anything you can think of is possible. What I would tell you is that you've got to have a process to reach higher. And don't stop once you reach great heights; ask what's next. You never know where something that seems impossible is going to lead you, and that's a beautiful thing. Sometimes you'll be pleasantly surprised by where life can lead you. Twenty-five years after leading Hardeeville as a teenager with barely any concrete career goals, I ended up as the head of military education for the air force. I ended up coaching and speaking on leadership. I didn't think one-tenth of that was possible twenty-five years ago. But every time I reached a milestone, I kept climbing—and I'm still climbing.

REFLECTION 5
DON'T READ YOUR OWN PRESS CLIPS

CHERISH YOUR ACHIEVEMENTS AND BE proud of everything you've built or accomplished. But don't settle into what you've done and assume it's the greatest you ever will do or be and that it's the end. Everyone is always chasing that MVP title or Super Bowl ring. Don't read the press clips and settle. Read the press clips and say you won that victory in that moment. Celebrate it, but don't look at it as the end. You've got to continue and avoid relishing in that moment as a finality. You have more to give, more to do, and more to learn.

On the flip side, I would say that you should not take the press clips other people write about you as a finality, either. If there is a lesson to take from them that will help you become better, then take it. But don't stop where they've pegged you.

REFLECTION 6
SHED THE WEIGHT

In order to be successful, sometimes you have to shed things that aren't good for you. It's just like going to the doctor and getting told you've got to lose weight for your health. The same thing happens in life. And it can be difficult. Extremely difficult. Sometimes the weight you've got to shed is unhealthy relationships—even family relationships. You may lose friends who were once close but are now doing more harm than good. You've got to look around and evaluate your circle, and this is one of the most difficult things to do. You have to assume that people who come into your circle may be in your life forever. And hopefully you want them to be. But the reality is, you have to know when someone is bringing you extra weight you can't take on, temporarily or permanently. You need to be cognizant of your own health and how much weight you are carrying from others.

REFLECTION 7
YOUR FINAL CHAPTER

You don't have to stop striving until the day you leave this Earth. You can keep looking for those *Why not me?* opportunities to live the life you want—to retire at fifty-five and live in the Caribbean, to run a marathon, or to get a PhD. Your final chapter is not written until you're six feet under the ground. So don't think your age or even a disability limits you. You can find ways around it and do what you want to do.

Your final chapter is only over when you can't control your destiny anymore. Until then, you can control your destiny about where you want to go. Don't limit yourself. Live every day with excitement and vigor. Once you're gone, the only thing you can hope for is that the legacy and inspiration you left for others will lead them well down their own path. And that's your final chapter.

FINAL REFLECTION
WHY NOT YOU?

I've asked that question many times in my life, but in a negative sense. In its many different gradations, the question really was: *Why can't I be more?* But I've learned—and come to believe so strongly that I want to share it with you—that you can also ask the same question from a place of empowerment. *Why not me?*

Remember, there will be challenges that come your way as you attempt to live out that question. But you can overcome them all if you don't give up. I think, above all, the theme of my life has been perseverance. I never gave up, and I don't want you to, either. You can write your own story—that's what I did.

Why not you?

Why not you for president? Why not you for a great dad or mom? For a great spouse? Professor? Doctor? Why not you for the best possible you? Why not you for whatever you woke up this morning wanting to achieve? Don't just ask that question—live it. Wake up in the morning and walk out that door feeling empowered to be the best you want to really be—the one you know you can really be in your heart.

Why not me? Why not you?

MILITARY CRISIS LINE

Connects active-duty service members and veterans in crisis with qualified and caring Dept. of Veterans Affairs responders through a confidential, toll-free hotline, 24–7. Support is available via telephone, mobile text, or online.

Crisis Line
veteranscrisisline.net
Call 1-800-273-TALK (8255, Option 1)
Text 838255

MILITARY ONESOURCE

Military OneSource offers free and confidential non-medical counseling via phone and live chat, 24–7. They also offer specialty consultations, with services including peer-to-peer support, wounded warrior support, health and wellness coaching, transition assistance, and more.

militaryonesource.mil
Call 1-800-342-9647 (CONUS)
CONUS - 703-253-7599 and follow local instructions for placing a collect call to the United States.

24/7 CRISIS HOTLINE

National Suicide Prevention Lifeline Network
suicidepreventionlifeline.org
1-800-273-TALK (8255) (Veterans, press 1)

CRISIS TEXT LINE

Text TALK to 741-741 to text with a trained crisis counselor from the Crisis Text Line for free, 24–7.

VETERANS CRISIS LINE

Send a text to 838255